THE VOYNICH MANUSCRIPT
"The Most Mysterious Manuscript in the World"

BY BRIGADIER JOHN H. TILTMAN

The Voynich Manuscript
"The Most Mysterious Manuscript in the World"

BY BRIGADIER JOHN H. TILTMAN

The following paper is a slightly expanded version of a paper which I delivered to the Baltimore Bibliophiles on March 4, 1967. I am fully aware of the inadequacy of my treatment of the subject. The paper is intended only as an introduction to the study of the manuscript for anyone approaching it for the first time.

INTRODUCTION

The Voynich Manuscript is a vellum book of over 200 pages. There is text on almost every page in an unknown script. There are also coloured drawings on all but about 20 pages.

Plate 1 will give you an idea of what the script looks like. *Plate 2* is an example of an illustrated page.*

To the best of my knowledge there is no confirmed solution of the script or any part of it, and the authorship and general dating of the manuscript is totally unknown. With the exception of a small number of later additions (not in the unknown script), the character of the script and general behavior of the symbols appear to be constant throughout the book. Opinions differ as to whether the whole is by one hand. There appear to be no erasures or corrections, which suggests that the manuscript as we see it is likely to be a copy of an original which may be of an earlier date. In any case the writing of the manuscript and the painting of the illustrations must have been a major undertaking. The late Father Petersen made his own transcription of the manuscript without the illustrations, and it occupied him for, I believe, three or four years.

Only a comparatively small part of this paper is original, i.e., has not appeared in print before. My purpose in writing it is to widen the circle of those who might be interested in the manuscript. I am a working man and have not been able to devote much time to its study and am fully aware of the many deficiencies in my knowledge.

DESCRIPTION AND HISTORY

In 1912 the manuscript was purchased by the late Mr. Wilfred M. Voynich (later a rare book dealer in New York) who "discovered it in

---

*All plates appear at the end of the article.

a chest in an ancient castle in Southern Europe." It is now owned by Mr. H. P. Kraus, the New York antiquarian bookseller, who has revealed that it was found at Mondragone. This is a villa in Frascati near Rome, built by Cardinal Altemps about 1570. In 1582 Pope Gregory XIII issued from Mondragone the bull reforming the calendar. The villa apparently continued in the Altemps family as in 1620 a later member of the family bequeathed the Mondragone library to the Vatican library. In 1865 the villa became a Jesuit college which was finally closed in 1953. From 1912 to 1919, Voynich attempted to interest scholars in Europe and America in solving the script, while trying himself to determine the origin of the manuscript.

The manuscript, when discovered, was accompanied by a letter, shown in *Plate 3*. With Mr. Kraus's permission I quote from his catalogue number 100, entitled *Thirty Five Manuscripts*, the passages "History of the Manuscript" and "Conjectures concerning the early history of the Manuscript:"

HISTORY OF THE MANUSCRIPT

The manuscript enters recorded history on the 19th of August, 1666, when Joannes Marcus Marci of Cronland sent the codex from Prague to Athanasius Kircher, at Rome, with a signed autograph letter, which is found loosely laid into the manuscript. It reads as follows (transl. from the Latin):

"Reverend and Distinguished Sir, Father in Christ:

"This book, bequeathed to me by an intimate friend, I destined for you, my very dear Athanasius, as soon as it came into my possession, for I was convinced that it could be read by no one except yourself.

"The former owner of this book asked your opinion by letter, copying and sending you a portion of the book from which he believed you would be able to read the remainder, but he at that time refused to send the book itself. To its deciphering he devoted unflagging toil, as is apparent from attempts of his which I send you herewith, and he relinquished hope only with his life. But his toil was in vain, for such Sphinxes as these obey no one but their master, Kircher. Accept now this token, such as it is and long overdue though it be, of my affection for you, and burst through its bars, if there are any, with your wonted success.

"Dr. Raphael, a tutor in the Bohemian language to Ferdinand III, then King of Bohemia, told me the said book belonged to the Emperor Rudolph and that he presented to the bearer who brought him the book 600 ducats. He believed the author was Roger Bacon, the Englishman. On this point I suspend judgement; it is your place to define for us what view we should take thereon, to whose favor and kindness I unreservedly commit myself and remain,

At the command of your Reverence
Joannes Marcus Marci
Of Cronland

Prague, 19th August, 1666."

The last numeral of the date has been altered by pen from "5" to "6," obviously by Marcus himself. The emperor Rudolf II (1552–1612) was a scholar rather than a man of affairs; he neglected his duties as ruler of his realm in order to devote

2

himself to the study of alchemy, astrology, and astronomy, and he was the patron of Tycho Brahe, Kepler, John Dee, and a host of other scientists and pseudo-scientists. He resided in Prague throughout most of his reign, where he assembled a great collection of books and art objects. Rudolf, after acquiring the book, apparently loaned or gave it to Jacobus Horcicky de Tepenecz (died 1622), whose name, "Jacobi à Tepenece," is written on the recto of the first leaf (erased, but easily visible under ultra-violet light). The form of the name shows that the book must have been in his hands after 1608, when the "de Tepenecz" was acquired by patent of nobility from the Emperor. Tepenecz was the director of Rudolf's alchemical laboratory and his botanical gardens.

Dr. Raphael (1580–1644), a lawyer and minor poet, who supplied information concerning the book to Marcus, was connected with the Imperial court under Emperors Rudolf II, Ferdinand II, and Ferdinand III, and thus was in an excellent position to have obtained knowledge concerning the codex. He was attorney-general of Bohemia under Ferdinand III.

Joannes Marcus (1595–1667), the writer of the letter, was Rector of the University of Prague, and a noted physician, mathematician, and orientalist. He was official physician to the Emperor Ferdinand III. In 1667 he was elected a corresponding member of the British Royal Society. He had studied under Kircher, at Rome.

The connection of the cipher manuscript with the famous Athanasius Kircher, S.J. (1601–1680), is especially intriguing. He was one of the foremost scholars of the Jesuit order, keenly interested in problems of decipherment and the author of three works on an attempted solution of the Egyptian hieroglyphics, and of another work (*Polygraphia*, 1663), on codes and ciphers in general. In the XXth century the codex was acquired by Wilfried M. Voynich, a dealer in manuscripts, in 1912, who discovered it in a chest "in an ancient castle in Southern Europe."

CONJECTURES CONCERNING THE EARLY HISTORY OF THE MANUSCRIPT

In his letter, Marcus says, "He (apparently the Emperor Rudolf) believed the author was Roger Bacon, the Englishman." Bacon (1214?–1294), famous scientist and philosopher of the Middle Ages, studied and taught at Oxford and Paris, and is believed to have died at Oxford. Professor Newbold, who considered this manuscript to be in the autograph handwriting of Roger Bacon, conjectured that his papers were acquired after his death by some English monastery; that the present one, on the dissolution of the monasteries after 1538, was acquired by John Dudley, Duke of Northumberland (1502?–1553); that John Dee (1527–1608) acquired it from the Duke or some other member of the Dudley family; and that Dee, who lived in Prague for several years and was personally acquainted with Rudolf II, sold it to him.

An interesting point is that John Dee, while in Bohemia from 1585 to 1588, possessed

"a book . . . containing nothing but hieroglyphicks; which book his father bestowed much time upon, but I could not hear that he could make it out"

(Sir Thomas Browne, quoting Dr. Arthur Dee, 1579–1651, the son of John Dee.). It is indeed very probable that the present volume was the one which Arthur Dee saw in his father's hands; it would seem from the tenor of this reference, that the elder Dee was trying to extract some meaning from the book. It is quite possible that the Emperor, after purchasing it, had entrusted it to him for decipherment. The word "hieroglyphicks" would not, of course, refer at the time to Egyptian writing specifically, but to any secret alphabet such as that of the present codex.

Plate 4 is a photograph of the bibliographical description of the manuscript in the Kraus catalogue.

In the manuscript there are 125 pages of botanical drawings, 26 of astronomical (or astrological drawings), 28 of so-called biological drawings, and 34 of pharmaceutical drawings, nearly all accompanied by text. At the end there are about 20 pages of script without illustrations. *Plates 5 to 15* show examples of the appearance of the pages.

Plate 5.—The plant depicted here has been identified as some sort of Bindweed (Convolvulus).

Plate 6.—This seems to me a fairly natural representation of cross-leaved Heath (Erica).

Plate 7.—This has been identified as sunflower, giving rise to the hypothesis that the manuscript cannot be dated earlier than 1493, when Columbus introduced sunflowers into Europe. This identification has not been universally accepted.

Plate 8.—This is an example of the many drawings which appear to be composite and cannot be identified as any one plant. I should perhaps apologise for the lack of definition in some of these illustrations. This one was prepared from my photostat which was reproduced from Mr. Friedman's photostat, which was itself a copy of a photostat made many years ago by Father Petersen.

Plate 9.—This is one of the astronomical illustrations.

Plate 10.—This is one of the so-called zodiacal illustrations. There were presumably either one or two for each month, but the pages for two months seem to be missing. For each month there are 30 (or about 30) human figures round the edge of the circle.

Plate 11 shows two pages for April. One page has a black bull and 15 unclothed ladies, and the other, a white bull and 15 clothed ladies. All the zodiacal drawings carry the name of the month in the centre in a later hand and in readable script though the language has been disputed.

Plate 12.—This is one example of the illustrations in the biological part of the book. I have not myself studied these pages, and ideas as to their meaning advanced by specialists in medieval and early Renaissance history are completely outside my field.

Plate 13.—This drawing is an example of one of many pages which seem to comprise a sort of pharmacopeia.

Plate 14.—This is the first page. There is no title page, but this appears to be a table of contents, there being four paragraphs corresponding to the four illustrated portions of the manuscript.

Plate 15.—This is the final page and has on more than one occasion been assumed to be a key to a cipher used for producing the text as we see it.   You will see that only one short passage is in the unknown script used for the rest of the manuscript and that there appears to be some evidence of Latin words and at the end an unfinished Old English or Old German sentence.

PROPOSED SOLUTIONS

There have been three published solutions, none of them generally accepted.

(1) William R. Newbold, professor of moral and intellectual philosophy at the University of Pennsylvania, began work on the manuscript in 1919 and in April 1921 announced that he had discovered the key to a cipher, that he was convinced that the author was Roger Bacon, and that he had decyphered portions of it.   He said that his decypherment proved that Roger Bacon had possessed both a telescope and a microscope, although history places the invention of these several centuries after his death, and further that one of the drawings depicted the great Andromeda Spiral Nebula, of whose existence he, Newbold, had been previously unaware.   His solution, which was accepted at the time by Voynich and a number of scholars, was eventually demolished, particularly by Professor John M. Manly, Chairman of the English Department of the University of Chicago, in an article "Roger Bacon and the Voynich MS.," *Speculum,* July 1931, and now has no supporters.   His complex method of decypherment (I quote from an article by Mrs. Friedman in the *Washington Post* of 5 August 1962) "was reducible to nine steps.   The first and last of these, without any consideration of the intermediate abstruse and confusing processes, are utterly devoid of precision and are incapable of yielding one and only one plain language text—a rigid requirement of any legitimate cipher method. His first step was to convert the individual strokes of each symbol into Greek shorthand, a process of which Newbold himself said: 'I frequently find it impossible to read the same text in exactly the same way.'   The reason for this, palaeographers say, is that what Newbold saw as separate strokes of a symbol are merely the results of the cracking, uneven spreading and fading of the ink, and the condition of the vellum because of the manuscript's age."   Newbold died in 1926, and two years later his literary executor published a full-sized book from his voluminous notes and worksheets—*The Cipher of Roger Bacon*.

Plate 16 is an illustration from his book showing his interpretation in the form of shorthand strokes of a letter of the script; the page illustrated is one of the astronomical drawings and the arrangement of the stars near the portion of script which the author has chosen for illustration suggests Aldebaran and the Hyades.

The controversy over Newbold's solution left a legacy of ill-feeling which persisted for many years and which I found reflected in a letter which Charles Singer wrote to me in 1957.

(2) In 1943 a Rochester lawyer named Feely published a book entitled *Roger Bacon's Cipher; The Right Key Found*. Feely was the author of some published items in the field of the Shakespeare authorship controversy. His unmethodical method produced text in unacceptable mediaeval Latin, in unauthentic abbreviated forms.

(3) In 1946, a research scientist, Dr. Leonell C. Strong, published a different interpretation of part of the manuscript. He claimed to have decyphered part of two pages, one of them the Sunflower page shown in *Plate 7*. He said that his decypherment revealed to him that the author was Anthony Askham and that the plain language text was in mediaeval English. Again his mediaeval English is not acceptable to scholars. He did not reveal the details of his key but his description of the cipher method makes no sense to cryptologists. However, in the process of preparing this paper I came across the following curious fact. Among the many editions of an illustrated English printed work known generally as *Banckes's Herbal*, the first dated 1525, are two usually attributed to Anthony Askham, dated 1550 and 1555. Their title pages read:—"A little herbal of the properties of herbs newly amended and corrected, with certain additions at the end of the book, declaring what herbs hath influence of certain stars and constellations, whereby may be chosen the best and most lucky times and days of their ministration, according to the moon being in the signs of heaven, the which is daily appointed in the Almanac, made and gathered in the year of our Lord God 1550, the 12 day of February by Anthony Askham Physician." The strange thing about this is that the astrological additions promised the reader, appear nowhere in either edition. Anthony Askham, a physician and clergyman, also published a number of almanacs. I managed to get a sight of one of these in a Library of Congress microfilm but found it only to be a Christian calendar on half a dozen pages.

In 1950 I was introduced to the manuscript by my friend, Mr. William F. Friedman, who gave me photostats of a few of the pages to work on, chiefly the unillustrated pages at the end. From these pages I made a preliminary analysis of the text, disregarding all but the most commonly occurring symbols. For purposes of the present paper, I have found it necessary to substitute for the symbols conventional and quite arbitrary letters and figures, as shown at the top of *Plate 17*, very similar to the system previously devised by Mr. Friedman for discussion of the problem with a study group which he brought together for a short time at the end of World War II. You will see that I have limited the number of symbols to 17. The second symbols which I have placed at positions 1, 2, 15, 16 and 17, I have treated, rightly or wrongly, as variant forms. As a result of my analysis I made a report to Mr. Friedman in 1951 of which the following is the gist (only slightly revised).

"(a) Following are some notes on the common behaviour of some of the commonly occurring symbols. I would like to say that there is no statement of opinion below to which I cannot myself find plenty of contradiction. I am convinced that it is useless (as it is certainly discouraging) to take account at this stage of rare combinations of symbols. It is not even in every case possible to say what is a single symbol and what is not. For example, I am not completely satisfied that the commonly occurring A has not to be resolved into CI or possibly OI. I have found no punctuation at all.

(b) DZ and HZ appear to be infixes of D and H within T. The variant symbol represented by E appears most commonly at the end of a line, rarely elsewhere.

(c) Paragraphs nearly always begin with D or H, most commonly in the second variant forms, which also occur frequently in words in the top lines of paragraphs where there is some extra space.

(d) G occurs quite frequently as the initial symbol of a line followed immediately by a combination of symbols which seem to be happy without it in any part of a line away from the beginning. Otherwise it occurs chiefly before spaces very frequently preceded immediately by 8. Hence my belief that these two have some separative or conjunctive function. (I have to admit, however, that G also seems sometimes to take the place of O before D or H (though rarely, if ever, after 4); this is particularly noticeable in some of the captions to illustrations in the astronomical section of the manuscript—these most commonly begin OD or OH and it is here that we occasionally see GD or GH.)

(e) I have tried, for convenience of handling, to divide words into what I call "roots" and "suffixes." This arrangement is shown at the bottom of *Plate 17*. Regarding the second type of suffix, some of the combinations are so rare that I have been uncertain whether to take any account of them at all. Some are very common indeed. It seems to me that each of these combinations beginning A has its own characteristic frequency which it maintains in general throughout the manuscript and independent of context (except in cases where two or more A groups are together in series, as referred to later). These A groups, e.g., AR or AIIL, frequently occur attached directly to "roots," particularly OD, OH, 8 and 2. ODAIIL, 4ODAIIL and 8AIIL rank high among the commonest words in the manuscript.

(f) There are however many examples of 2, 3, 4 or even 5 A groups strung together on end with or without spaces between them. When this occurs, there appears to be some selective preference. For example, AR is very frequently doubled, i.e., AR AR, whereas AIIL which is generally significantly commoner, is rarely found doubled. Perhaps the commonest succession of three of these groups is AR AR AE. AE very frequently follows AR, but AR hardly ever follows AE.

(g) O, which has a very common and very definite function in "roots," seems to occur frequently in "suffixes" in rather similar usage to A, but nearly always as OR and OE. OR AIIL is very common.

(h) The behaviour of the A (and O) groups has suggested to me that they may in fact constitute some form of spelling. It might be, for instance, that the manuscript is intended to demonstrate some very primitive universal language and that the author was driven to spell out the ends of words in order to express the accidence of an inflected language. If all the possible A and O combinations can occur, then there are 24 possibilities. They may, however, be modified or qualified in some way by the prefixed symbols D, H, OD, OH, T, S, 8, 2, etc., and I have not so far found it possible to draw a line anywhere. This, coupled with ignorance of the basic language, if any, makes it difficult to make any sort of attempt at solution, even assuming that there is spelling.

(i) E, usually preceded by A or O, is very commonly followed by D, much less commonly by H, with or without a space between. In this connection, I have become more and more inclined to believe that a space, though not intended to deceive, must not necessarily be regarded as a mark of division between two words or concepts.

(j) Speaking generally, each symbol behaves as if it had its own place in an "order of precedence" within words; some symbols such as O and G seem to be able to occupy two functionally different places.

(k) Some of the commoner words, e.g., ODCCG, ODCC8G, 4ODCC8G, ODAIIL, ODAR, ODAE, 8AIIL, TC8G occur twice running, occasionally three times.

(l) I am unable to avoid the conclusion that the occurrence of the symbol C up to 3 times in one form of "suffix" and the symbol I up to 3 times in the other must have some systematic significance.

(m) Peter Long has suggested to me that the A groups might represent Roman numerals. Thus AIIL might be IIJ, and AR AR AE XXV, but this, if true, would only present one with a set of numbered categories which doesn't solve the problem. In any case, though it accounts for the properties of the commoner combinations, it produces many impossible ones.

(n) The next three plates show pages where the symbols occur singly, apparently in series, and not in their normal functions. The column of symbols at the left in *Plate 18* appears to show a repeating cycle of 6 or 7 symbols D (or H), O, 2, G, C,?. In *Plate 19* the succession of symbols in the circles must surely have some significance. One circle has the same series of 17 symbols repeated 4 times. *Plate 20* also has an interesting column of symbols. In all three there are symbols which rarely, if ever, occur elsewhere.

(o) My analysis, I believe, shows that the text cannot be the result of substituting single symbols for letters in the natural order. Languages simply do not behave in this way. If the single words attached to stars in the astronomical drawings, for instance, are really, as they appear to be, captions expressing the names or qualities of those stars, there can hardly be any form of transposition system involved. And yet I am not aware of any long repetitions of more than 2 or 3 words in succession, as might be expected for instance in the text under the botanical drawings."

After reading my report, Mr. Friedman disclosed to me his belief that the basis of the script was a very primitive form of synthetic universal language such as was developed in the form of a philosophical classification of ideas by Bishop Wilkins in 1667 and Dalgarno a little later. It was clear that the productions of these two men were much too systematic, and anything of the kind would have been almost instantly recognisable. My analysis seemed to me to reveal a cumbersome mixture of different kinds of substitution. When I was attempting to trace back the idea of universal language, I came upon a printed book entitled *The Universal Character* by Cave Beck, London 1657 (also printed in French in the same year). Cave Beck was one of the original members of the British Royal Society and his system was certainly a cumbersome mixture.

Plate 21 shows the title page. His system is based on a dictionary code of about 4,000 words to which are alloted the numbers from 1–3999 in alphabetical order.

Plate 22 is a page from his dictionary covering the words "That (conjunction)" to "till or untill." When digital code-groups are unaccompanied by letters, they represent verbal infinitives, e.g., "to tickle"-3773. Groups are preceded by the letter R when a noun is indicated as in the case of most of the groups on this page; if the adjectival form is intended, the digital group is preceded by Q. In the case of words which the author regards as synonymous with words earlier in the alphabet, the earlier code-group is given, e.g., "to thinke"-1163, where "to cogitate" is found on an earlier page opposite 1163. Prepositions are represented by the corresponding word in Latin, e.g., "through"-*per*. Some very common words have trigraphic equivalents beginning S and T to be found in a separate list of about 175 such words; these are repeated in their alphabetical place in the main dictionary, e.g., "that"–SNA. There are also on this page "thou"–E, "thine"–HE, and "this"–HO; also "Thursday"–+5 1484, i.e., "number five day." Plurals are designated by placing the letter S immediately after the digital code-group. There are also many other circumstances, particularly in the case of parts of verbs, which necessitate the prefixing of up to three letters before the digital code-group as the example taken from Cave Beck's book shows (*Plate 23*). As each word or concept treated as a word consists generally of a combination of letters and digits, it is necessary to put a comma after it to delimit it. I have wondered whether G and 8G in the Voynich Manuscript might be accounted for as representing "comma" and "plural comma." (I am aware that 8 occurs in other contexts in the manuscript, but so does S in Cave Beck's system.) Curiously, in his example (*Plate 23*) his substitution for "days" is given as 14848, not 1484S, as one would have expected.

Cave Beck starts his preface as follows: "This last century of years, much has been the discourse and expectation of learned men, concerning the finding out of an universal character . . . . . ." If this is to be taken literally, it carries the idea of universal language back to about the middle of the 16th Century. I tried in 1957 to trace back the idea of universal character, but I had little time to devote to this research and the earliest evidence I was able to find is contained in the following extracts from two lives of Bishop Bedell, who died in 1642, one by Burnet, dated 1692, and the other by Clogy, dated 1682, referring to a man named Johnston.

> "But the Bishop finding the man had a very mercurial wit, and a great capacity, he resolved to set him to work, that so he might not be wholly useless to the Church; and therefore he proposed to him the composing of an universal character, that might be equally well understood by all nations: and he showed him, that since there was already an universal mathematical character, received for Arithmetick, Geometry and Astronomy, the other was not impossible to be done. Johnston undertook it readily and the Bishop drew for him a scheme of the whole work, which be brought to such perfection that . . . he put it under the Press, but the Rebellion prevented his finishing it."
>
> "My Lord gave him a platform which he observed; all the difficulty was about the syncategoramata. He styled his books with spell. I heard that some part of it was printed; but the rebellion prevented finishing."

It would seem that these events cannot be dated later than 1641.

It is, however, difficult to date the manuscript anywhere near as late as this. Charles Singer, in a letter to me, put the date at late 16th Century. Professor Panoffsky and the keeper of the manuscripts at the Cambridge Library both independently insisted on a date within 20 years of 1500 A.D., and the manuscript as we have it may be a copy of a much earlier document.

HERBALS

At this point I propose to undertake a short digression on the subject of manuscript and early printed herbals. This may be thought irrelevant and my treatment will certainly be very superficial, but, if the plain text of the Voynich manuscript belongs to the illustrations on the same pages, as we have a right to expect in the complete absence of evidence to the contrary, then much the greater part of that text is related to plants. However, I have to admit that to the best of my knowledge no one has been able to find any point of connection with any other mediaeval manuscript or early printed book. This is all the stranger because the range of writing and illustration on the subject of the plant world from the early middle ages right through into the 16th and even 17th centuries is very limited indeed.

The first significant name is Krateuas, the Rhizotomist (rhizotomist meaning "root-digger") who was body physician to Mithridates VI Eupator, the King of Pontus who was defeated by Pompey and took his own life in 63 B.C. Krateuas wrote a herbal in which plants were not described but were depicted in figures which were followed by brief discussions of the medical uses of plants. Some of this herbal has been preserved by Dioscorides who was a physician attached to the Roman army in Asia about the middle of the first century A.D., and who is much the most famous name as a herbal writer in classical times. He wrote in Greek the work usually known as *De Materia Medica*. One of the most beautiful and, I imagine, the most valuable manuscripts in existence is the so-called Juliana Anicia codex at Vienna, written about 512 A.D. for presentation to Juliana Anicia, whose father was for a short time western Roman Emperor in 472 A.D. Two facsimiles of this manuscript have been published, the second in five parts, of which the first two are in the Garden Library at Dumbarton Oaks. Part of the manuscript is a text of Dioscorides, and the whole is magnificently illustrated in colour. I have reproduced here in *Plates 24 and 25* two pages of the manuscript. Charles Singer, in a most interesting article in the British *Journal of Hellenic Studies* for 1927, has restored about ten of the original drawings of Krateuas from it.

Plate 26 shows Krateuas engaged in painting a Mandrake held by Epinoia, the genius of Intelligence, while Dioscorides beyond writes in a book. This representation of mandrake as a nude figure, male or female, with leaves sprouting from or replacing the head, persists in illustrated herbals into the era of early printed books and even into the 17th century, carrying with it a collection of superstitions, some of them to do with the precautions to be taken when digging it up.

In 1957 I paid visits to a few specialists in early herbals in England. Among them I saw the late Dr. T. A. Sprague in Cheltenham and showed him a few specimen photostats of herbal drawings from the Voynich manuscript, of which he had been previously unaware. As he looked at them he became more and more agitated and eventually said

> "Do you know what you are asking me to do? I have spent the last twenty years of my life trying to identify the plant drawings in the Juliana Anicia codex when the names of the plants are given in Greek, Latin and usually Arabic, and you are asking me to identify these awful pictures."

One of the earliest illustrated printed herbals was the Herbarium of Apuleius Platonicus (printed in Rome about 1481) with Latin text. (This is not the Apuleius who wrote *The Golden Ass*). Virtually nothing is known of him, but his work is believed to have been originally written in Greek about 400 A.D. There are many extant manuscripts of it, including a finely illustrated translation into Anglo-Saxon about 1050 A.D., now in the British Museum.

But the three main herbal Incunabula, all originally printed in Mainz, are the Latin *Herbarius*—1484, the German *Herbarius*—1485, and *Ortus Sanitatis*—1491. This latter also appeared in translation as *Jardin De Sante* and *Gart Der Gesundheit*. There is a good facsimile of the German *Herbarius*. The woodcuts from all these are all rather stylized, obviously not drawn from nature.

Plate 27 is a typical illustration from the Latin *Herbarius*.

Plate 28.- I couldn't resist introducing this as a lighter note. It shows the woodcut of Narcissus from *Ortus Sanitatis* beside Lear's "Manypeeplia Upsidownia" from his *Nonsense Botany*.

Plate 29 was prepared from a copy of *Ortus Sanitatis* at Dumbarton Oaks, showing the female Mandrake picture and the text that goes with it.

A new era in the history of the herbal may be said to date from 1530 when the first part of *Herbarium Vivae Eicones* was published in Strassburg. This is known as Brunfels' herbal, and in it the plants are represented as they are. *Plate 30* shows a woodcut from this book.

Throughout the texts of all the early printed herbals (and presumably their forerunners in manuscript) runs the theme of the four elements and their natures—fire, hot and dry—air, hot and moist—earth, cold and dry—water, cold and moist. For instance, in the German *Herbarius* one finds on nearly every page a sentence such as "A finds this plant of the second degree of coldness and the third degree of dampness, but B considers it of the third degree of coldness."

In general, the illustrations in the early printed herbals are limited to two or three collections of stylized woodcuts copied over and over again in more and more degenerate form. The same superstitions persist. Probably the most fantastic is the story of the Barnacle Tree. According to one version, trees sprout from the wood of shipwrecks, shells grow at the ends of the branches, and from the shells small geese gradually emerge and fly away.

Plate 31 is taken from Gerard's herbal—1597. Gerard claims to have seen this process in action with his own eyes on a small island in Lancashire.

I make no apology for this short survey of herbals. I repeat that my purpose is to interest a wider circle, and the text and illustrations of herbals of the 13th, 14th, and 15th Centuries are a most interesting part of the background of this odd book. To the best of my knowledge no one has seen any book, certainly no illustrated book, of the period which covers the wide range suggested by the drawings in it.

There are many aspects of the study of the manuscript which I have not covered in this paper. Little has been said about Roger Bacon, very little of John Dee, nothing at all of such figures as Ramon Lull. There is as yet no solid evidence that the manuscript is not by Roger Bacon or a copy of a work by him.

BIBLIOGRAPHICAL NOTE

|1| W. R. Newbold (edited by R. G. Kent), *The Cipher of Roger Bacon*, University of Pennsylvania, 1928. This book was published after Professor Newbold's death from his notes and would probably not have been published at all had he lived longer since, after the first announcement of his decipherment of parts of the Voynich Manuscript, Newbold made virtually no progress at all. In spite of the fact that his solution is now quite unacceptable, the earlier part of this book should be read by anyone interested as it provides a more comprehensive background than any other source.

|2| Agnes Arber, *Herbals, Their Origin and Evolution*, 1470–1670, second edition, Cambridge, 1953. This is the standard work on the history of herbals.

|3| Robert T. Gunther, *The Greek Herbal of Dioscorides*, Hafner, 1959. The text of this book is an early English translation of *De Materia Medica* of Dioscorides, very fully illustrated with line drawings traced from the illustrations of the Juliana Anicia manuscript.

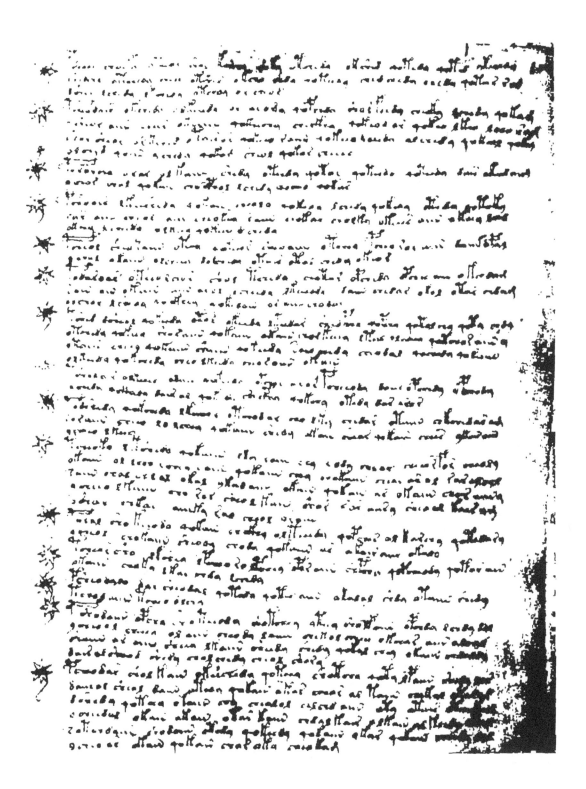

Plate I.

J. H. TILTMAN

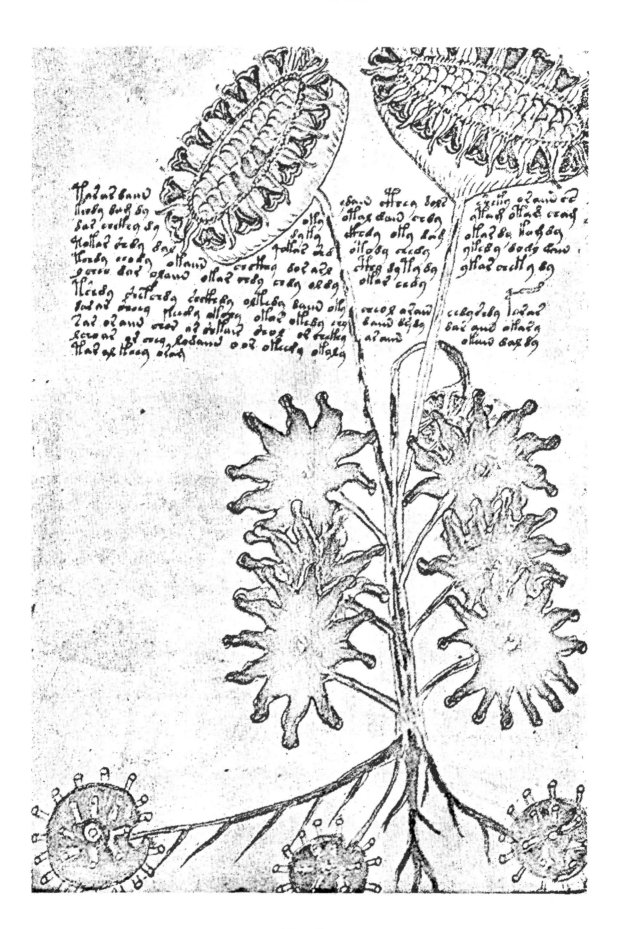

Plate 2.

VOYNICH MANUSCRIPT

Reuerende et Eximie Dñe
in Christo Pater

Librum hunc ab Amico singulari mihi testamento relictum, mox
eundem tibi amicissime Athanasi uti primum possidere cœpi, animo des-
tinaui. Siquidem persuasum habui â nullo nisi abste legi posse. Petiji
aliquando per litteras ejusdem libri tum possessor judicium tuum parte
aliqua libri â se descripta et tibi transmissa. ex qua reliqua â te legi
posse persuasum habuit; uerùm librum ipsum transmittere tum recu-
sabat, in quo discifrando posuit indefessum laborem, uti manifestum ex
conatibus ejusdem hic una tibi transmissis neg prius hujus spei quàm
uitæ suæ finem fecit. uerùm labor ille frustraneus fuit, siquidem non
nisi suo Kirchero obediunt eiusmodi sphinges. accipe ergo modo quod
pridem tibi debebatur hoc qualecunq mei ergâ te affectus indicium,
huiusq seras ei arcana, consueta tibi felicitate perrumpe. retulit mihi
D. Doctor Raphaël Ferdinandi tertij Regis tum Boëmiæ in lingua boëmica
instructor dictum librum fuisse Rudolphi Imperatoris, pro quo ipse latori
qui librum attulisset 600 ducatos præsentarit, Authorem uerò ipsum pu-
tabat esse Rogerium Baconem Anglum. ego judicium meum hic sus-
pendo. tu uerò quid nobis hic sentiendum defini, cujus fauori et gra-
tiæ me totum commendo maneôq

Rtiæ Vestræ

Ad obseruandum

Joannes Marcus Marci
a Cronland

Pragæ 19. Augusti
1665.

Plate 3.

J. H. TILTMAN

"THE MOST MYSTERIOUS MANUSCRIPT IN THE WORLD"

THE ROGER BACON CIPHER MANUSCRIPT

(BACON, ROGER ?.) Cipher manuscript on vellum. Text written in a secret script, apparently based on Roman minuscule characters, irregularly disposed on the pages. 102 leaves (of 116; lacks 14 leaves), including 7 double-folio folding leaves; 3 triple folio folding leaves; and one quadruple folio folding leaf. With added signature marks (of the XVth or XVIth century), and foliation (of the XVIth or XVIIth century) 1-11, 13-58, 65-73, 75-90, 93-96, 99-108, 111-116. With about 400 drawings of botanical subjects, including many of full-page size; 33 drawings of astrological or astronomical subjects, plus about 350 single star-figures; and 42 (biological?) drawings, most of which include human figures. The drawings colored in several shades of green, brown, light yellow, blue, and dark red. Large 8vo (c. 230 × c. 160 mm.). Old limp vellum covers (now detached). From the libraries of John Dee (?), the Emperor Rudolph II (reigned 1576-1611); Jacobus Horcicky (Sinapius) de Tepenecz; Joannes Marcus Marci of Cronland (1666); Athanasius Kircher, S. J.; and Wilfrid M. Voynich. Accompanied by an Autograph Letter signed by Joannes Marcus, presenting the book to Athanasius Kircher.

No place or date, (XVth century, or earlier?).

An enigmatic mediaeval manuscript, which for over forty years has baffled the scholars and cryptographers who have attempted to wrest its secrets from it. It has been termed by Professor John M. Manly, who made a detailed study of it, "the most mysterious manuscript in the world."

Plate 4.

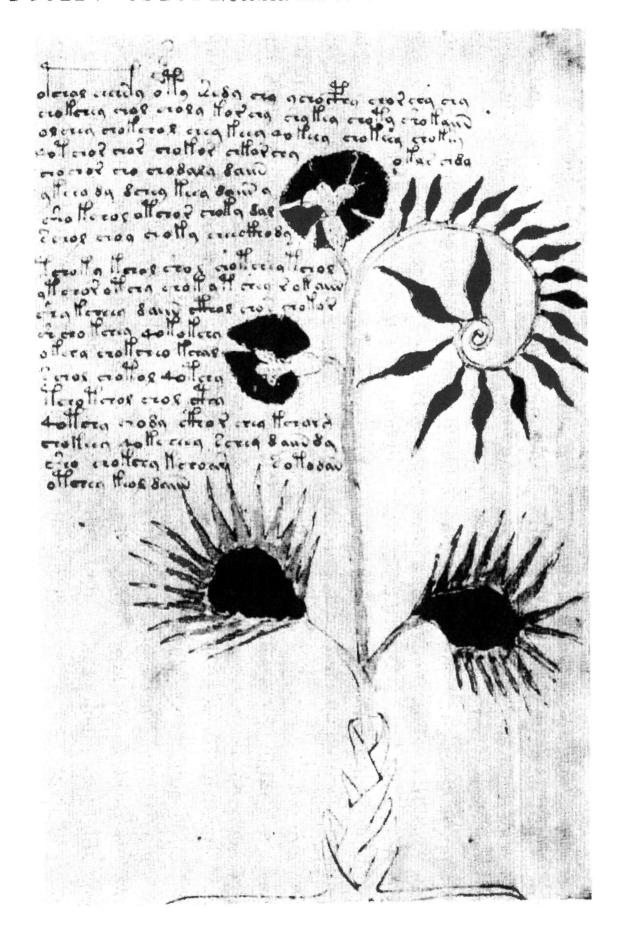

Plate 5.

Plate 6.

Plate 7.

Plate 8.

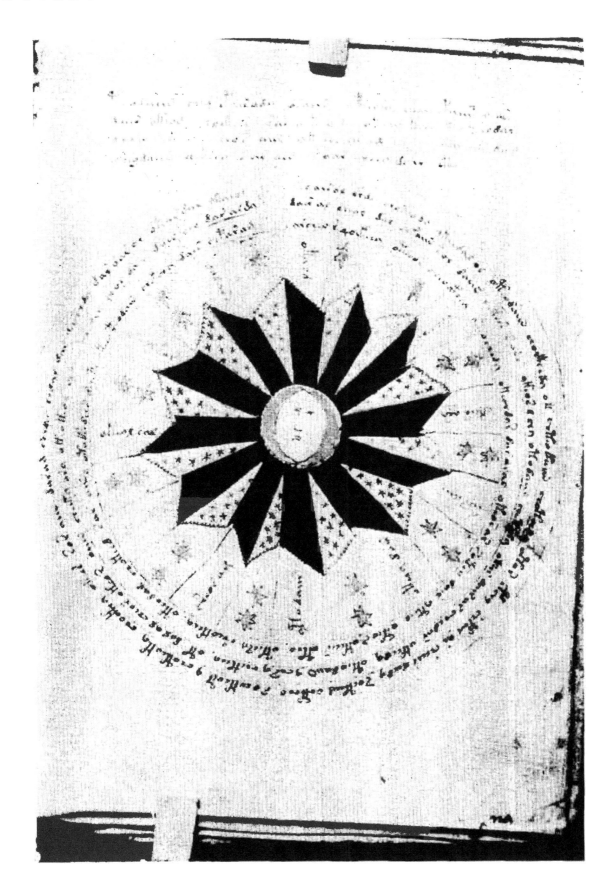

Plate 9.

Plate 10

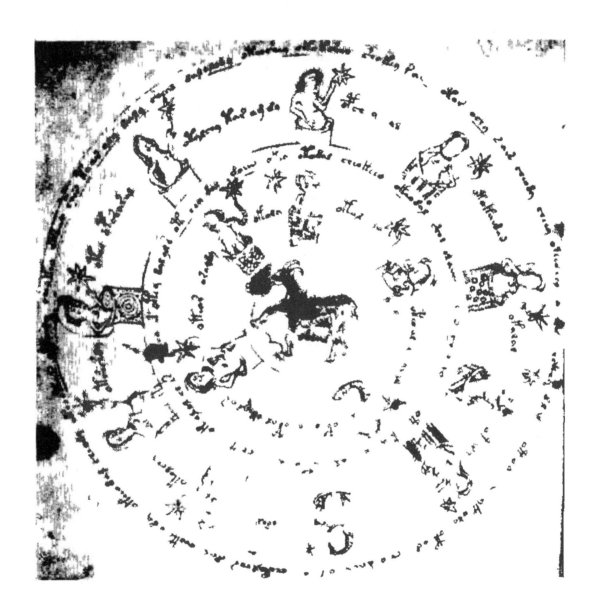

Plate 11a

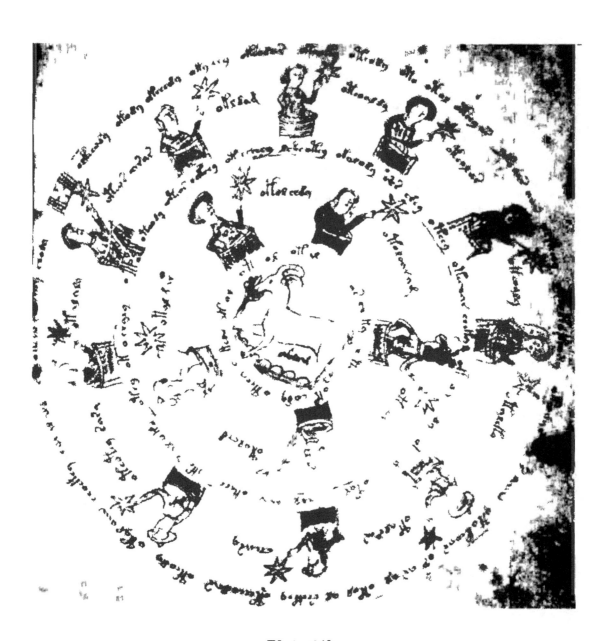

Plate 11b

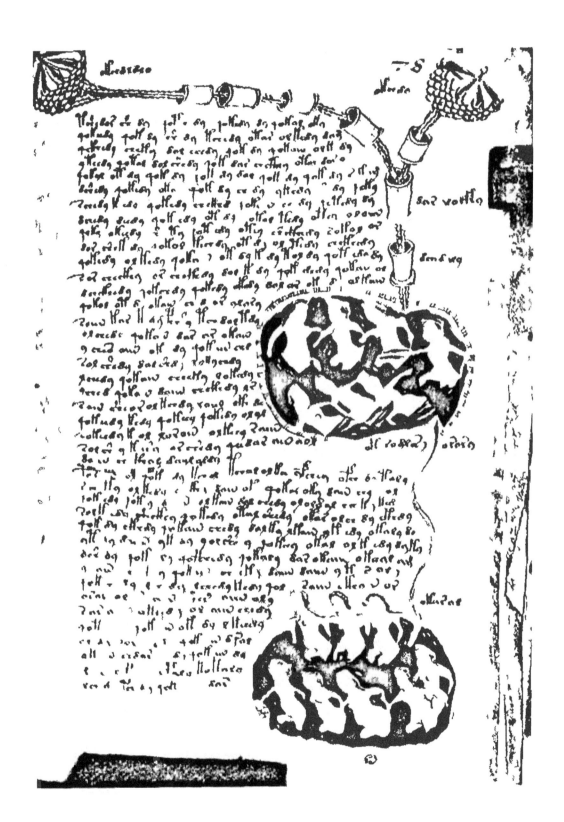

Plate 12

Plate 13

Plate 14.

Plate 15

J H TILTMAN

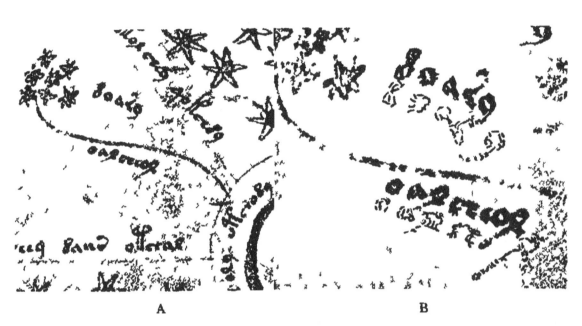

A   B

Part of folio 68 recto in various enlargements A is enlarged about two diameters and B about four diameters   After a certain amount of enlargement the characters lose definition but the drawings of the microscopic characters by Newbold in B look probable

Plate 16

J H TILTMAN

GDOCAIIL SBCG 4ODAE EDC8G 4ODC8G
4ODC8 4OBC8G ODAET8ARAETAR-AIIL
UNGTCCORAIIL ODCCGTCOETC8G OHTC8
OHTC8G AEDC8G AEEDCAEOE2AILAE
UPAIR ODAETC8G 4ODCC8G OHCORAE
4ODC8G 4ODC8G GDAIIL OHC8AR
TAEDCC8G
UIGTC8AILOR-TCD8G 4OAIIL ODCCG
4ODCCG T8AE ODC8G 4ODC8G ODC8AE
T8G
U2AIEAROEDCCG AOAEOEDC8G OEAIIL
OHOETC8G ODC8G 4CHTC8G ODOEOEDCG
HDC8G 4OHAIIL OHC8G ODCC8G
OHO8AE
UODCOETC8AE TODC8G C4ODC8G OHTC8G
2AIILAEDAL

Preliminary division of very common words into 'roots' and
suffixes –
Roots   OD, OH, 4OD, 4OH, T, S, 8, 2, ED
Suffixes   either (I) C, CC, CCL followed by G or 8G
            or (II) one or more of the following –
                A–   AIL   AIIL   AIIIL
                AR   AIR   4IIR   AIIIR
                AE   AIE   AIIE   AIIIE
                OR   OE

Plate 17

31

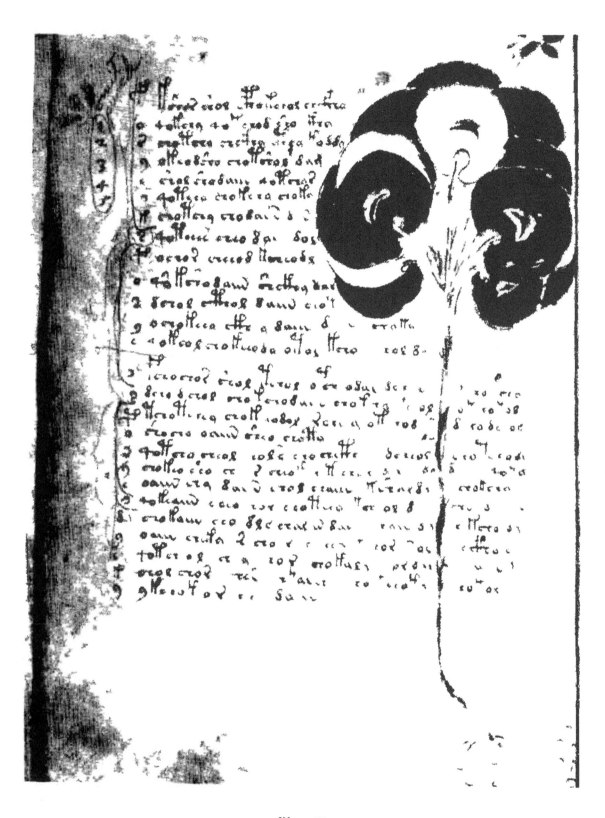

Plate 18

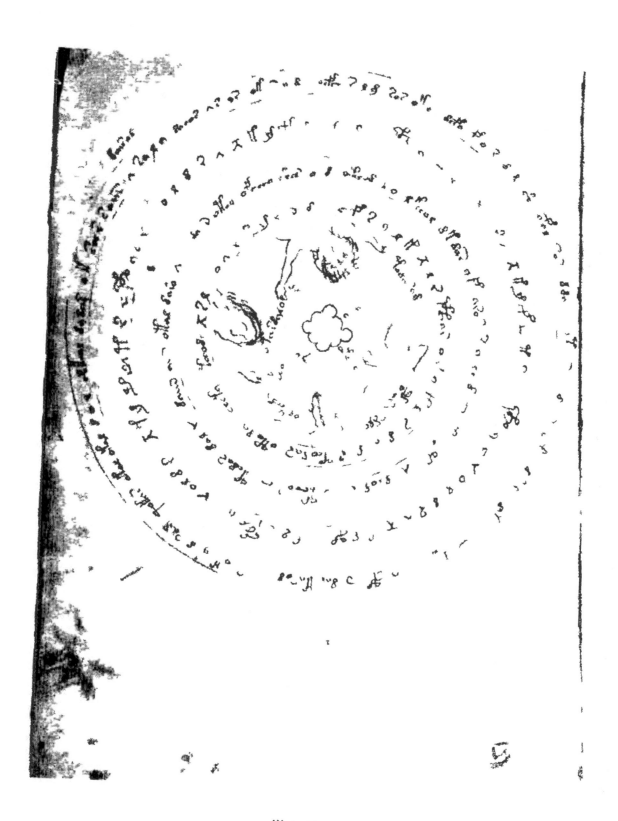

Plate 19

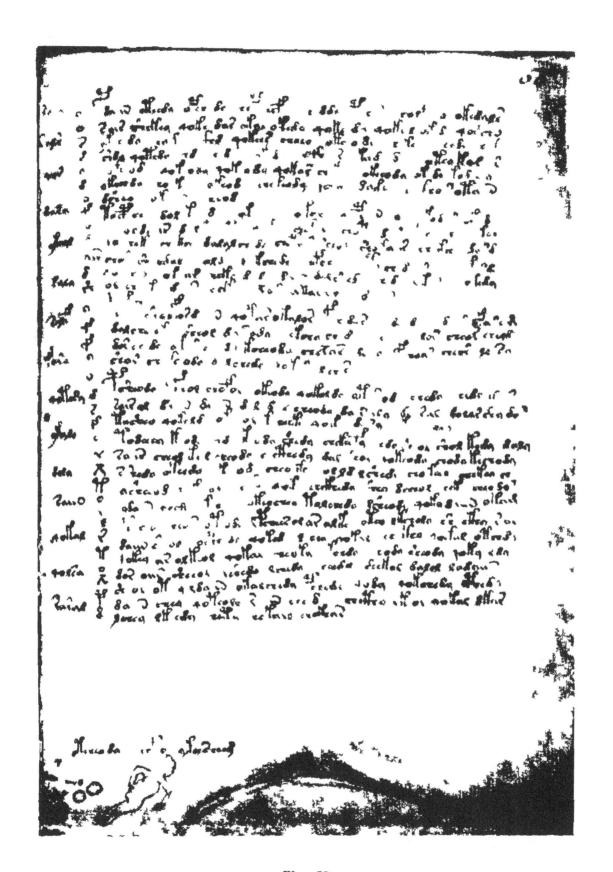

Plate 20

THE UNIVERSAL
CHARACTER,

By which all the Nations in
the World may understand
one anothers Conceptions,
Reading out of one Common
Writing their own
Mother Tongues.

AN
INVENTION
Of GENERAL Use,

The Practise whereof may be Attai-
ned in two Hours space, Observing the
GRAMMATICAL Directions.

Which CHARACTER is so contri-
ved, that it may be Spoken as well
as Written.

By *Cave Beck,* M.A.

LONDON,
Printed by Th. Maxey, for *William Weekley,* and
are to be sold at his shop in *Ipswich.* 1657.

Plate 21

35

that conjunct	sna	to threaten	1215
to thatch	3757	to thresh	1923
to than, no	1267	to thrive, v. grow	
a theater, tam	480	thrift or frugality t	2016
a theefe p	1745	the throat r	874
then adverb of time	sni	a throne r	2436
then in comparison	sno	to throb	116
thence	snu	to throng, v. Crowd	1399
Theology r	1606	a threstle bird	3769
therefore	spa	to throw or cast	927
there	sne	thrummes	r 3770
a Thesis	3182	a thrush bird	r 3771
thicke q	802	to thrust	1400
the thigh	r 3758	a thumbe, +	1907
a thiller of a Cart	r 3759	to thumpe or knocke	673
a thimble	r 3760	a thunderbolt, sure	624
thinne q	312	thunder r	624
thine	he	Thursday +5.	1484
a thing r	2069	to thwack, ant	508
to thinke	1163	thyme herb	r 3772
to thirst	1654	to tickle	3773
this	ho	the tide	r 3774
a thistle	r 3761	tidings	r 3775
thither	spe	to tye or binde	302
a thong	r 3762	tiffany	r 3776
a thorne	r 3763	a tiger	r 3777
a white thorne	r 3764	a tick of a bed	r 3778
a blacke thorne	r 3765	a tick worme	r 3779
a thorne-backe fish	r 3766	a tile	r 3780
a thorpe or village	r 3767	a gutter tile or roofe tile	
through	per		r 2197
thou	e	to till or allure	138
thraldome r	626	to till the ground	1422
thread	r 3768	till or untill	spa
threadbare or old	208	a till	

Plate 22

36

An Example of writing and speaking the fifth Commandement.

Honour thy Father and thy Mother

Write { leb 2314   p 2477 and pf 2477

Speak { leb toreónfo, pee tofofénfen, & pif tofofenfen

That thy days may be long

fna, her 14848   mb 1716

fna heronfórafos, mib onfenónfic

In the Land which the Lord

in p 1699   vip 2529

in ponlicnínnin   vip tohtónin

Thy God giveth thee

hep 306   pce b 510

hep tréofic   pee behóno

* Note, for Euphony fake or the better found, the letter [t] in [tre] may sometimes be left out and [t] in [at] may for the same caufe be omitted or changed into the Confonant following as onfórafo or onforaffo, which liberty is ufually taken in all languages as Commend for Conmend affemble for affemble.

L A U S D E O.

Plate 23

37

Plate 24

J H TILTMAN

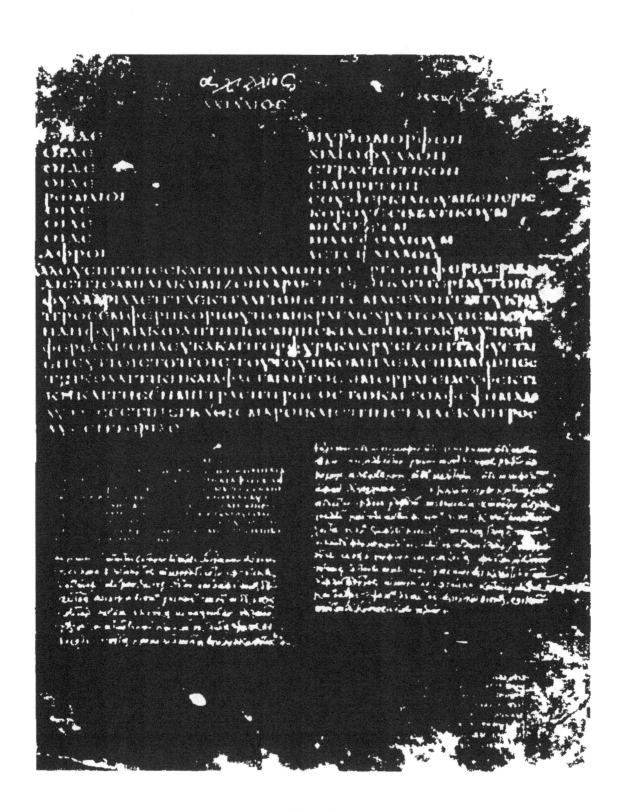

Plate 25

FIG 3—TRACING FROM THE JULIANA ANICIA CODEX OF 512, Fo 5 v

Epinoia holds a mandrake in her hand. Krateuas is painting it while Dioskurides
writes an account of it in a codex In the original figure much of the paint has
scaled off and our restoration is conjectural in places

Plate 26

BRIONIA

Fig 6 "Brionia [*Latin Herbarius* (Arnaldus de Villa Nova,
Tractatus de virtutibus herbarum), 1499]

Plate 27

41

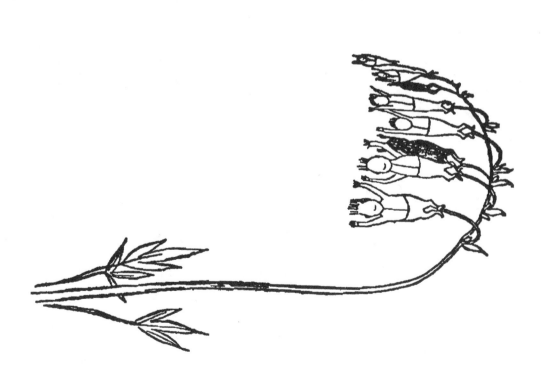

Plate 28

VOYNICH MANUSCRIPT

J. H. TILTMAN

Plate 29.

43

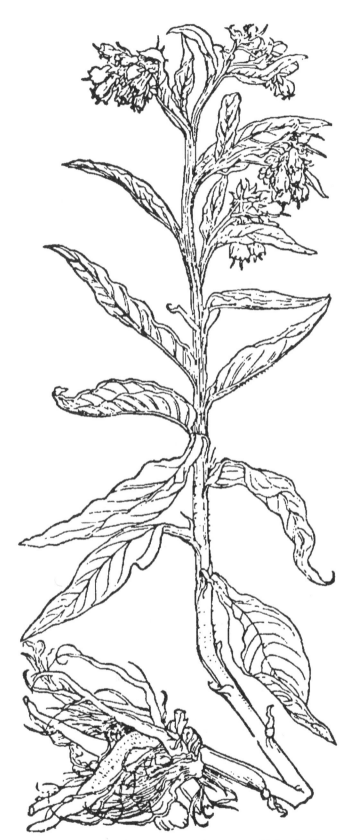

Fig. 22. "Walwurtz männlin", *Symphytum officinale* L., var. *purpureum*
Pers., Comfrey [Brunfels, *Herbarum vivae eicones*, vol. 1, 1530] *Reduced*

Plate 30.

The breede of Barnakles.

Fig. 60. "The breede of Barnakles" [Gerard, *The Herball*, 1597]

Plate 31.

An Application of PTAH to the Voynich Manuscript (U)

BY MARY E. D'IMPERIO

Top Secret Umbra

(U) This article is the second in a series of studies applying some modern statistical techniques to the problems posed by the Voynich manuscript. This study attempts to discover and demonstrate regularities of patterning in the Voynich text subjectively noted by many earlier students of the manuscript. Three separate PTAH studies are described, attacking the Voynich text at three levels: single symbols, whole "words," and a carefully chosen set of substrings within "words." These analyses are applied to samples of text from the "Biological B" section of the manuscript, in Currier's transcription. A brief general characterization of PTAH is provided, with an explanation of how it is used in the present application.

(U) The author draws the following general conclusions: (1) The plain text directly underlying the Voynich text is probably not a natural language written in an alphabet, like English or Latin. (2) The Voynich text probably does not involve any form of simple substitution or alphabetic plain text like English or Latin. (3) The Voynich text probably does not directly represent a variably spelled or "impressionistic" approximation of a natural language like English or Latin, as claimed by Brumbaugh. (4) The words of the Voynich text do not appear to act like code groups in a known code which includes groups for grammatical endings.

1. INTRODUCTION (U)

(U) This article is the second in a series of studies applying some modern statistical techniques to the problems posed by the Voynich manuscript. The first article described an application of cluster analysis and multidimensional scaling [4]. Like that earlier paper, this paper is also intended to serve a tutorial purpose, in explaining how the techniques can be applied to a complex and interesting problem, in the hope of aiding others to apply them in operational contexts. I will not burden the reader with a description of the Voynich manuscript, since I presume most are by now familiar with the general nature of this cryptanalytic puzzle that has come down to us from the late Middle Ages. For any reader desiring more background, I recommend the proceedings of our 1976 Seminar [5], a copy of which may

NSAL-S-215,957

be obtained from M. D'Imperio, R53/P13. Many readers will also recall the informative and enjoyable presentation by Brigadier John Tiltman on 17 November, 1975.

(U) One of the most frustrating aspects of the Voynich text is its contradictory nature, from the point of view of the analyst. On the one hand, it is highly repetitive, so as to appear at times almost like the "babbling" of many closely similar words in succession (in a manner reminiscent of the refrains of some folk songs or nursery rhymes). This repetitious character has led some to propose that the text might have been generated by some "psychological random" process, as a dummy production to cover some hidden message. Some have even suggested that it may be the product of a mentally disturbed person, who invented the strings of symbols in a form of echolalia, or "speaking in tongues," so that their meaning, if any, is likely to be irrecoverable.

(U) On the other hand, the text has a very clear and consistent structure that is readily apparent to the student as soon as he begins to examine a page. The occurrence of words within lines and symbols within words exhibits the operation of orderly rules, most of which appear to hold throughout the very long and voluminous manuscript, and others of which appear to hold throughout all of certain subsections (as pointed out by Currier, and supported by our cluster analysis results). Certain sequences of symbols recur in similar parts of words consistently; some symbols regularly occupy preferred positions at the beginnings, middles, and ends of words, and at the beginnings and ends of lines; some symbols appear frequently before or after other symbols, and rarely elsewhere. Monographic frequency distributions, regardless of where in the text they are sampled, are very rough. What is more, most symbols retain the same relative frequency of occurrence throughout the lengthy text, with the exception of a few symbols whose frequency seems to vary from subsection to subsection in the "language" contrasts found by Currier. This curious combination of apparently senseless repetition of words with structural regularity of symbols within words poses a very puzzling challenge to the analyst. It is hard indeed to imagine what manner of plain text could be hidden in symbol strings exhibiting these characteristics, if any form of simple substitution is proposed.

(U) William F. Friedman and Brigadier Tiltman have studied the regularity of occurrence of symbols within words in the Voynich text, and have tried to elucidate and exploit the "beginning-middle-end" structure they perceived. A code-like system, with page numbers in sections (all the plant names, parts of the body, star names, etc. together on adjacent pages), might account for the repeated "beginnings" of words. Coded grammatical endings based on Latin, and perhaps including some encipherment of Roman numerals (within their repeated "c" and "i" symbols) might account for the "endings" and "middles." In fact, many code-like systems of this kind were in use by the

Catholic Church during the fifteenth and sixteenth centuries. Early versions of universal or international artificial languages, based on Latin and showing a similar code-like structure, were a favorite preoccupation of scholars in the seventeenth and eighteenth centuries; their ancestry can be traced back to still older mnemonic systems used by the Church and having their ultimate origin in the practices of Roman orators. (For a much more detailed discussion of these topics, see my forthcoming monograph [6]). Friedman and Tiltman hypothesized that an artificial language of this kind might underlie the Voynich text.

(C-CCO) I have also found this code or artifical language theory highly attractive as a way of explaining the strange contradictions pointed out above. So far, however, no student has been able to devise a means of confirming or invalidating the theory, or even of clearly demonstrating the intuitively striking regularities of structure in the text. The present study is an attempt to discover and display those regularities, if any, present in a sample of text from one section of the Voynich manuscript, analyzing it at three levels of structure: using single words, and parts of words as units in three separate studies. The statistical tool I chose for the analysis is the PTAH technique of statistical modelling.

2. PTAH (C-CCO)

(C-CCO) PTAH (named for the Egyptian god of wisdom), is a general statistical method developed at IDA (Institute for Defense Analyses), Princeton University. According to Angela Boyter's excellent paper in the *NSA Technical Journal* [2], PTAH got its name when a programmer, Mr. Gerry Mitchell, was listening to the opera "Aida" while working on his program. He was struck by the passage "immenso Ptah noi invociam," and named his program after the Egyptian god. The name was ultimately extended from this program, implementing a particular application of the method, to the method and its mathematical theory as well [2, p 85]. According to [   ] of R51, the name is pronounced "however you like" [8]. The technique itself and its uses are classified Top Secret Codeword.

I chose PTAH for the present study for two main reasons: first, because of the applications of PTAH to book codes, and second, because I wished to learn more about PTAH itself [   ]

(U) I will make no attempt here to explain "how PTAH works." The documentation seems, with a few exceptions, to fall in two classes: one clearly oriented toward mathematicians, and presenting very heavy going indeed for others; and another describing a specific application and providing little or no insight into PTAH itself or the rationale of its use in the given case. As a nonmathematician, I cannot hope to understand the first class of papers on PTAH, let alone attempt to explain their concepts in simple words meaningful to prospective users with an application in mind. Since this article is aimed at such prospective users, I will restrict my remarks on PTAH to a general attempt to characterize the machine runs and analyses that were made in this study, and to provide some flavor or the approach a user might take to his problem and his data in order to prepare input to the PTAH computer programs and interpret their output. I strongly recommend the paper by   [2], which is a notable exception to my plaint above concerning documentation. The following paragraphs of explanation are based entirely on her clear and helpful exposition. I wish also to express my sincere appreciation for the aid of   of PI, who made the computer runs in support of this study and assisted me in planning the analyses and interpreting the findings.

(C CCO) The explanations of PTAH provided in the papers for nonmathematicians employ examples involving urns filled with slips of paper on which letters, or some other observable events, are recorded. The PTAH "model" is like a conceptual "machine" whose behavior is adjusted to simulate the observed behavior (as expressed in a long sequence of letters or other unitary events of interest) produced

(C CCO)

(b)(1)
(b)(3)-50 USC 403
(b)(3)-18 USC 798
(b)(3)-P.L. 86-36

(b)(3)-P.L. 86-36

(U) PTAH is iterative, i.e., it cycles repetitively through its calculations until it achieves the best approximation to the events it is simulating, as judged by statistical tests. At the start, we guess at a number of states to try in the model, and arrive at the best number by trying several models of varying sizes and seeing which appears to fit the data best. We provide the programs with a string of text (which may need to be edited to get at arbitrary units other than single letters, *n*-graphs, or words). We prime the program with initial probabilities to start off the two sets of "urns"—the "transition matrix" for the states, and the "output matrix" for the outputs. These initial probabilities can be chosen at random, so long as they add up to 1 for each row of the transition matrix and each column of the output matrix. As the program runs, it changes the probabilities a little on each cycle until the results seem to be converging on the set of values most likely to have produced the input text sample. Having created this statistical "machine" in the form of the two matrices, we could now demonstrate it if we wished by another program which causes it to manufacture new text according to its probabilities. [   ] provides an example of artificial "English" text produced in this way by a 12-state PTAH model of single letters [2, p. 93]. PTAH is different from other models, such as the digraphic probability model, in that PTAH provides the best model of the data along the entire stream, not just digraph by digraph; it "remembers" more about the system it is simulating.

(U) All of the PTAH program runs made by [   ] for all three phases of this study contained the following displays: 1) an initial transition matrix representing the starting probabilities for the iterative process; 2) frequency counts of the units (letters, words, word-parts) being studied, ranked by descending frequency; 3) a set of scores for each iteration to aid the PTAH expert in assessing how well the process is converging on an optimum result; 4) transition matrix after a given number of iterations; and

5) output matrix after that number of iterations. Several intermediate matrices are provided; the results probably of most interest to the user are 6) the final transition matrix, 7) the final output matrix, and 8) several listings of "clusters" at thresholds of decreasing restrictiveness, which show smaller sets of relatively similar elements within those associated with the states.

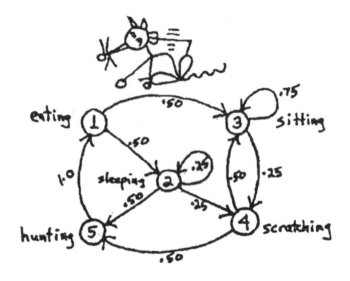

State Transition Diagram (U)

		Successor State				
State	Label	1	2	3	4	5
1	Eating	—	.50	.50	—	—
2	Sleeping	—	.25	—	.25	.50
3	Sitting	—	—	.75	.25	—
4	Scratching	—	—	.50	—	.50
5	Hunting	1.0	—	—	—	—

Transition Matrix (U)

UNCLASSIFIED

Fig. 1—Behavior of a Mythical Animal (U)

3. APPLICATIONS TO THE VOYNICH MANUSCRIPT (U)

(U) Researchers have seen apparent regularities in the Voynich text on various levels of structure; patterns have been seen in sequences of single "letters," sequences of words, and sequences of parts within words. Accordingly, with [   ] aid, I decided upon a three-pronged attack on the Voynich text on these three levels. Each of the resulting three separate studies will be described separately in the paragraphs below, and the findings of each presented.

(U) 3.1 *Analysis of Single Voynich Symbols.* A sample of 3313 consecutive "letters" was chosen from the "Biological B" Section of the manuscript, converted to machinable form by means of Capt. Prescott Currier's transcription. This transcription, as may be seen from Fig. 2a, already includes some combinations of from one to four smaller elements (e.g. "M" = *//ſ*, "U" = *//v*.) which Currier found to be almost invariably linked to form an apparent unit. I chose the "Biological B" pages for my sample because they have been shown (originally by Currier and also in my cluster analysis study) to be more homogeneous and to display a stronger statistical identity than any other section of the manuscript. The extreme roughness of the monographic frequencies is apparent in Fig. 2a. Since Currier and others have found that certain symbols occur more often at the beginnings and ends of words and lines, I included an arbitrary symbol for "end of word" and another for "end of line" in the analysis. Including these, a total of 28 different symbols occurred in the sample, comprising 554 "words" in 67 lines of text. The text sample was fed into the PTAH programs, which generated the frequency counts of symbols ranked in order of descending frequency as an initial step in the analysis.

(U) Figure 2b shows the "Final Transition Matrix" for five states produced by the PTAH programs after 70 iterations. The programs can be set up to produce other numbers of states, depending on the guesses the researcher may have about the structure of his text. In this case, since we knew nothing to start with about the Voynich script and its alphabet, five states were chosen because that number has often proven useful in other studies. Each "state" is associated with one of five subsets of the Voynich script symbols. The decimal numbers in the cells of the matrix are probabilities that the state for that row, and its associated set of symbols, will be followed by each of the states (and sets of symbols) in the columns. The characters assigned by the analysis to each of the states may be seen in Fig. 2b below the matrix. I have also suggested an intuitive verbal label for each state. Each state represents a set of Voynich symbols that seem to act alike in their contacts with other symbols within the text. Figure 2c shows a "state transition diagram" — a graphic representation of the information in the transition matrix. Arrows lead from each state to the other states most likely to follow, and are labelled with the respective probabilities.

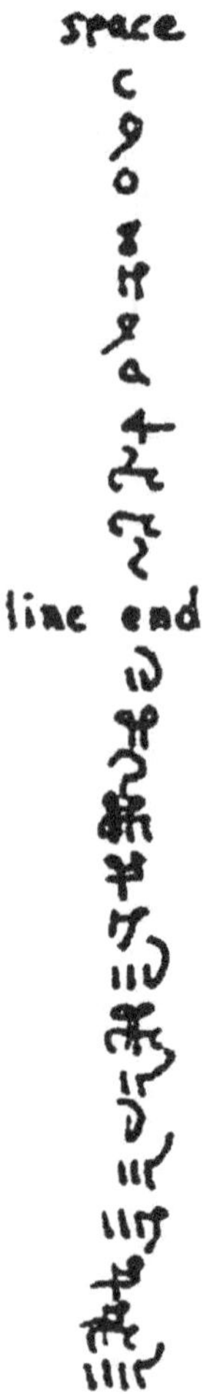

Transcribed symbol	Voynich symbol	Frequency	Rank
1	space	554	1
c		378	2
9		365	3
o		355	4
8		273	5
f		216	6
e		191	7
a		186	8
4		181	9
z		110	10
s		105	11
r		98	12
↓	line end	67	13
n		64	14
p		60	15
2		32	16
x		17	17
b		16	18
j		12	19
m		11	20
q		6	21
t		5	22
d		4	23
u		3	24
I		1	25
v		1	26
y		1	27
0		1	28

UNCLASSIFIED

Fig. 2a—Monographic Frequencies and Ranks (U)

(U) With due apologies to any purists, mathematical or otherwise, who may be reading this paper, I will present a frivolous and over-simplified example in an attempt to get across the flavor of the PTAH model, and the import of the matrices and other displays in Fig. 2. Let us imagine an animal that can exhibit five major kinds of activities (or most of whose life can be adequately described in terms of five sets of behaviors). He can eat, sleep, hunt for food, sit still, and scratch for fleas. By counting a long sequence of actions in the animal's life, we can arrive at an idea of which sets of actions he is likely to do, in which order. If we see him hunting, we know he is most likely to be eating next; after eating, he will either sleep or sit still; after sleeping he will either scratch fleas or start hunting again, and so forth, like an automatic washer going through its cycle. We presume that, underlying these five major sets of common behaviors, the animal has five internal states: an eating, sleeping, hunting, sitting, and scratching state. (Since all we see are his actions, and we cannot get "inside his head," the best we can do in labelling the states is to call them after the strongest or commonest action or characteristic of the event-set associated with each state.) Figure 1 shows a state transition diagram for the "five-state model" of the animal and the "transition matrix" on which the diagram was based.

State Transition Matrix (U)

	1	2	3	4	5
1	.1176077	.0000000	.0097794	.8610576	.0115553
2	.9731800	.0000000	.0049215	.0218984	.0000000
3	.0525056	.9474944	.0000000	.0000000	.0000000
4	.6234602	.0358985	.0260699	.0228168	2917546
5	.0297188	.0745607	.6002830	.0000000	.2954375

Static State Probabilities

.3520302 .1124551 .0921134 .3098980 .1335033

State Output Characters and Suggested Labels (U)

State	Label	Associated Voynich Symbols
1	"beginners-1," "separators"	word-space, o, a, line-end, v
2	"enders"	9, m, t, l, u, 0
3	"pre-enders"	8, x, q
4	"beginners-2," "post-beg.-1"	f, e, 4, r, n, p, 2, b, j, d
5	"middles"	c, z, s, y

UNCLASSIFIED

Figure 2b (U)

(U) Our way of looking at the "letters" of the Voynich text, in Fig. 2, is similar to our view of the mythical five-state animal. The state transition diagram in 2c shows the probabilities of the different states associated with the letters in 2b. I have shown only those arrows (likely movements from one state to another) with the highest probabilities, leaving out all those under .10 (representing changes to be expected in less than one tenth of the cases). We can summarize the import of Fig. 2 somewhat as follows:

a. State 1 is a "beginning" state, including my arbitrary characters for word-end and line-end and certain others that often follow immediately to start a word. It has a high probability of being followed by state 4 (secondary beginners) and most of the remaining time is followed by itself (i.e., a state 1 character following another state 1 character: typically end-of-line or end-of-word, then a word-beginning symbol.)

b. State 4, a secondary beginning state, is very likely to be followed by state 1 again (representing many common short "words"); otherwise, it is followed by state 5, a "middle" state. The two states 1 and 4 together account for most word-initial patterns of letters throughout the text.

c. State 5, the "middle" state, is most likely to be followed by state 3, which I call a "pre-ending" state for reasons to be seen below; otherwise, it is followed by another state 5. This state accounts for the "middles" of words—primarily the sequences "c, cc, ccc, sc, zc" which commonly come between the initial patterns and the "endings" proper.

d. State 3 seems to be a "pre-ending", or penultimate state, because it has a .95 probability of being followed by state 2, the "ending" state. (The small number of remaining cases of changes out of state 3 are to state 1, the beginning of a new word, with .05 probability, probably occasioned by the symbol "8" for the most part, which often precedes the ending "9" but sometimes occurs alone at the end of a word.)

e. State 2 is clearly an "ending" state, for word-final patterns; it is followed by State 1, the word-initial state, with a .97 probability. It is interesting to note that most of the few remaining cases are transitions to state 4, the secondary word-initial state; I would hazard a guess that these are cases where the text "words" were incorrectly separated in the transcription, so that the word-separator symbol was ommited.

(U) I will not attempt to describe here the output matrix or all the cluster displays for single Voynich symbols. My main use for the output matrix was to identify the letters associated with each of the five states. Involved in the interpretation is the frequency rank of each letter, as well as the probability it has in each state column. A letter which occurred only 5 times in 331 characters of text, but which had a 1.0 probability of being seen in a given state, may or may not be significant (the letter "Q" might be a somewhat similar case in English, being rare and almost always beginning words). On the other hand, a letter which occurred 500 times in the same text, and had a probability of .8 or .9 for one state is interesting in quite another way:

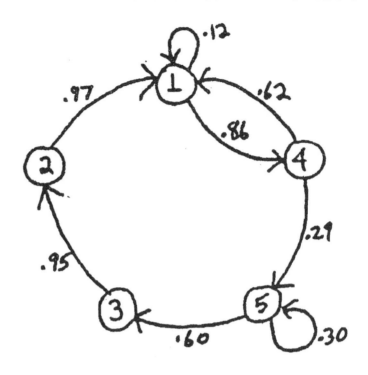

UNCLASSIFIED

Fig. 2c—State Transition Diagram

A (enders)
l, u, 0, 9

B (beg.-1)
a, o, v, line-end

C (beg.-2)
d, e, j, n, r, 4

UNCLASSIFIED

Fig. 2d—Clusters (threshold = .0010) (U)

These interpretations are embodied in the list of characters associated with the states in Fig. 2b. The "clusters" were generated by the program by analysis of the values in the final output matrix. Figure 2d shows these for the most restrictive threshold (.001). Their meaning is problematical, and I venture no interpretation. Half of the letters involved are very low in frequency, the other half very high.

(U) *Conclusions for the Single Letter Analysis.* It seems quite clear to me that the view exposed by Friedman and Tiltman concerning the positional structure within Voynich text words is strongly supported by these results. The Voynich symbols do indeed fall into well-defined classes associated with beginnings, middles, and ends of words. In addition, there is a mechanical, regimented quality about the picture we see here—an appearance of surprising orderliness, a highly limited and regular behavior and a resultant degree of predictability. All this seems to me most unlike what one would expect in a simple substitution on any natural language alphabet in running plain text.

(U) Let us compare the situation in Fig. 2 for Voynich symbols to that found by Cave and Neuwirth in a 5-state model for a very large sample of single letters in English text [3]. Figure 3a shows the transition matrix, a state diagram, and the letters assigned to each state. First we note that the diagram contains far more arrows, and has a cluttered look compared to our diagram for the Voynich symbols, made in exactly the same way (leaving out probabilities below .10). The diagram for Voynich symbols shows only eigth significant transitions, while that for English letter shows thirteen. Then we may see that it is much harder to characterize the sets of letters for each state; state 3 seems to concern vowels and "H," and state 5 is for the word spacer alone. The other states are hard to label, and do not relate in any clear and unequivocal way to position within words, except for state 4, which is followed most often by word space and seems to be a word-final state. State 1 contains most of the consonants, and is most often followed by state 3 for vowels and h. Nowhere do we see the positional regularity of beginners to middles to enders to new beginners that is so striking in Fig. 2. For a very complete and interesting analysis of various PTAH models of English, the reader is urged to consult the referenced paper, which is quite readable for the nonmathematician.

(U) The reader may well raise an objection here, pointing out that English is not an inflected language. It makes little use of grammatical affixes (prefixes, endings, etc.) in forming words, as do inflectional languages such as Latin or Russian. Even though the positional structure we have seen in the Voynich symbols looks nothing like that in English letters, might it not look more like the structure in Latin (which is considered by many students to be a likely language to seek in the Voynich text because of its universal use by medieval scholars)? With this reasonable question in mind, I asked [   ] to make a PTAH run for a five-state model of some Latin text,

Five-State Model for English Single Letters (U)
(adapted from Reference 3, p. 10)

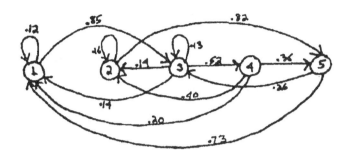

UNCLASSIFIED

State Transition Diagram (U)

State	Associated English Letters
1	t b c j m k p v z w q
2	s y e d g
3	a o h i u
4	n r f l x
5	word space

UNCLASSIFIED

Figure 3a (U)

4700 characters in length, from *Magia Naturalis*, by Giovanni Battista Porta, 1644 (a work concerned with materia medica, medical spells, natural "wonders," and such matters which seem related to the apparent content of the Voynich manuscript as evidenced by the drawings). In fact, the text I chose contained a series of prescriptions and instructions for preparing and administering herbal recipes to cure various diseases, and so should be closely comparable to the "Biological B" section of the Voynich text.

(U) Figure 3b shows the results of this analysis. While not quite as complex as that for English, the Latin diagram still has a lot more arrows and a much more intricate set of interconnections than that for Voynich symbols (eleven arrows as compared to eight). State 3 is the word separator; state 4 seems to contain many word-final letters which are last letters of common endings (-um, -us, -is, -ur, etc.); and state 1 contains some vowels that form these common endings. State 2 seems to show many word-beginning consonants. State 5 is an odd mixture of vowels "a" and "e," which also enter into common endings, and a conglomeration of odd consonants. While we can see reflections of the grammatical structure of Latin in the state diagram, we can find nothing like the clear positional structure evident in the Voynich symbol diagram of Fig. 2c. We can find little support for an attempt to explain the positional orderliness so clearly apparent in Voynich symbols within text "words" by referring them to Latin prefixes or endings in monographic plain text.

(U) I find the above comparisions quite convincing support for a view that the Voynich text, regarded as a string of single letters, does not "act like" natural language. Instead, it exhibits a clear positional regularity of characters within words. I believe that these findings strengthen the theory of Friedman and Tiltman that an artificial language may underlie the Voynich text.

(U) 3.2 *Analysis of Voynich Text Words.* My second study examines the behavior of whole words in the text, using the presence of spaces and end of line as indications of word separations. (It should be pointed out that the determination of "word" boundaries is often difficult in the Voynich manuscript, and some students have questioned the reliability of spacing as an indication of separate words. The transcription of our text sample, although made with great care by Currier, may have been mistaken as regards word separation in some unknown proportion of cases. The strength of the "beginning" and "ending" states in the first study just described may serve to reassure us that the space is indeed meaningful in separating units of structure, whatever they may be, and that the transcription was accurate for the most part in recognizing the boundries.) A sample consisting of 5567 apparent "words" in 764 consecutive lines was chosen, again from the "Biological B" section of the manuscript in Currier's transcription. A five-state PTAH analysis was run by _____ of P1, using "words" as units.

(U) Figure 4a shows the final transition matrix after 100 iterations, and provides a list of the strongest words for each of the five states, with a suggested label or characterization of each state, in terms of the composition of the words and the apparent relationships among the states. Only those words were included which had both frequencies of 10 or higher, and also probabilities greater than .6 of occurring in their assigned state. A state diagram may be seen in Fig. 4b. It is apparent that there are many transitions (13 in all as compared to 8 in Fig. 2c). There are three reciprocal

(b)(3)-P.L. 86-36

Five-State Model for Latin Single Letters (U)

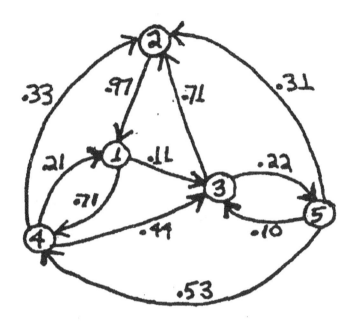

UNCLASSIFIED

State Transition Diagram (U)

State	Label	Associated Latin Letters
1	Pre-ender vowels?	y u i o
2	Beginner consonants?	z g v h t c d j
3	Word Space	word space
4	Ender consonants?	x m n r l s
5	?	f p e b g a

UNCLASSIFIED

Figure 3b (U)

transitions (state pairs for which state A can lead to state B, but B can also lead back to A again to form a little loop); there is only one such pair in the diagram for single letters. Thus, the diagram for words seems much more complex that that for letters, which is not really too surprising.

Voynich Text Words: Final Transition Matrix, Iteration 100 (U)

	1	2	3	4	5
1	.001312	.326610	.445735	.226324	.000018
2	.000013	.601243	.078920	.319821	.000003
3	.596741	.000001	.222830	.180226	.000202
4	.000000	.104757	.002946	.000000	.892297
5	.550690	.177433	.264313	.000372	.007192

Static State Probabilities (U)

.204763	.274850	.198561	.168628	.153198

Summary of Outputs and Major Features of States (U)

State	1	2	3	4	5
Features	z/s final 9	f/p, final 89	final a/o ending	end of line	line initial words
Output Words	am	oefcc89	r	/ / /	8sc89
	zcx9	4opc89	fan	(end	2or
	zq9	ofc89	oefan	of	8zc89
	zcc89	opc9	oeor	line	eoe
	zcc9	4ofc89	or	symbol)	psc89
	sq9	opc89	4ofar		zx9
	scf9	89	ofan		bsc89
	zc89	ezc89	ar		4ofs89
	zc9	oefc89	opam		2an
	scx9	4ofcc89	oe		8an
	sccf9	4opae	4ofan		2ae
	zcf9	oezc89			
	scc9				
	oesc9				

UNCLASSIFIED

Figure 4a

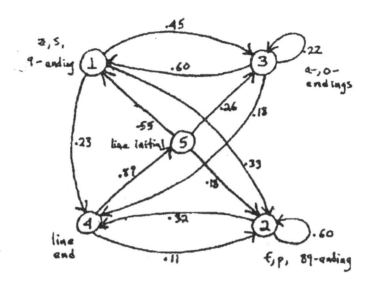

UNCLASSIFIED

Fig. 4b—Voynich Text Words: State Diagram (U)

(U) We may sum up the information in Fig. 4 as follows:

a. State 4 is associated with the line-ending symbol. It leads with a probability of .89 to state 5, which seems to consist of line-initial words, and with a probability of .11 to state 2.

b. State 5, as we have just seen, appears to be for line-initial words. Half of its high-frequency, high-probability words start with "2" or "8," a feature not seen in the word-lists for any other state. It is followed by state 1 with a .55 probability, state 3 with .22, and state 2 with .18.

c. State 3 exhibits a large number of words with "a" and "o" endings (AR, AM, AN, OR, OE); these are rare in the lists for any other state except state 5. It leads to state 1 with a .60 probability, to itself with .22, and to state 4 with .18.

d. State 1 shows many words ending in "9," with an initial or central "z" or "s," and a medial "c" or "cc." It leads to state 3 with probability .45, state 2 with .33, and state 4 with .23.

e. State 2 appears to involve many words ending in "89," having a central "f" or "p," and a medial "c" or "cc." It is followed by itself with probability .60, and by state 4 with .32.

f. The situation for line-final words is not as clear-cut as that for beginnings of lines. State 2 leads to the line-ending state 4 with probability .32, state 1 with .23, and state 3 with .18.

(U) *Conclusions from Analysis of Whole Words.* It seems strikingly clear that there is a positional structure of words within lines in the Voynich text, and that certain sets of words, with characertistic beginnings, middles and endings, are most likely to follow or precede certain other sets of words, with different beginnings, middles and endings. Currier has pointed out these two features of the text [5, pp 65-66]. Our analysis clearly supports both his view of the lines as functional entities, and his finding that words with certain endings were more likely to be followed by words with certain beginnings within a line. This is strange behavior indeed for any running plain text, unless it represents lists of parallel phrases (incantations? instructions? recipes?) in highly stereotyped form. Alternatively, the plaintext units underlying the "words" may not be natural language words but instead numbers or code groups of some sort, subject to some positional constraints. In any case, this curious characteristic of the Voynich text remains to be explained by any would-be decipherer; it does not appear to have been addressed by any of the claims known to me.

~~(TSC)~~ Since one of the theories about the Voynich text views it as possibly concealing a code-like system, let us compare the results of a five-state PTAH analysis applied to a

(U) 3.3 *Analysis of Word parts.* The analysis of repeating patterns of letters within words appears to me to provide the strongest and most interesting results of the three studies. The word parts, which I will call simply "strings" in what follows, were chosen by me on the (admittedly subjective) basis of my own experience on working with large volumes of text over several years, and in accordance with Tiltman's theories on "beginning" and "ending" patterns in words. I made up an initial list of about 50 strings, (shown in Appendix 1), which was used in the first of two PTAH analyses applied to word-parts. In this list I tried to include pairs of symbols that seemed related or similar in form and behavior ("s" and "z," "p" and "f," etc.). I also tried to anticipate and avoid conflicts in the resolution of letter

(1)
(3)-50 USC 403
(3)-18 USC 798
(3)-P.L. 86-36

)(3)-P.L. 86-36

sequences wherever possible. [_____] very kindly ran a pre-editing program on the input text to find and isolate all the strings on my list, leaving other character sequences as "left overs" that were also counted as elements in the analysis. To make this clearer, let us imagine that we were "parsing" the English phrase "now/is/the/time/" using strings "no," "is," "/," "the," and "me": the result would be "no w / is / the / ti me /," with ten product strings, two of which ("w" and "ti") are leftovers. As in the other studies, word-space and line-end were represented by arbitrary symbols, and I included them explicitly in my string list. A very large volume of text was entered, comprising 13,464 strings, in 3680 words, on 490 consecutive lines of "Biological B" data. A five-state PTAH model was used.

(U) Figure 6 shows the transition diagram and states for the first string list. 225 different elements were isolated in all by the pre-editing program; 99 of these, having frequencies of five or higher, were included in the analysis. The diagram in Fig. 6 shows a surprisingly simple structure, having eight transitions with probabilities of .10 or more. My interpretation can be summed up as follows:

a. State 1 is for word-separator and line-ending. It is followed by state 2 with probability .73, and by state 3 with .25.

b. State 5 is for word-endings. It leads to the separator state 1 with probability .96.

c. State 4 is the "middle" state. It exhibits only the special sequences of one, two, or three "c's" in a row, and the related sequence "c8." (It should be remembered that these "c8's" are only those not involved in a sequence of "c" followed by "89," which would have been split in that way.) State 4 is followed by the ending state 5 with probability .93.

d. State 3 I call the "beginners-1" state. It shows a special set of beginner strings, many associated with very common short words. It leads to the separator state 1 with probability .73, and to state 2 with .18.

e. State 2 is the "beginners-2" state. It produces a large list of strings starting longer words, some few of which can also follow certain of the "beginners-1" strings. It is followed by the ending state 5 with probability .60 and by the middle state 4 with .39.

f. Beginnings of words are shown by the successors of the separator state 1. They are, predictably, state 2 with probability .73 and state 3 with .25 (the two "beginner" states).

(U) In examining the complete list of strings produced by the pre-editing program and the "cluster" lists found in the PTAH analysis, I was struck by the recurrence of certain strings in the "leftovers." I collected an additional list of possible word parts to be added to the list, and also included all single letters, to force complete decomposition of "leftovers" in a new study. Appendix 2 shows the new characters and sequences. Since the pre-editing program looked for the longest matches first, the additions should have the effect of greatly shortening the list of elements in the study. With the new list, the elements found in the text should comprise only those sequences specified plus single symbols, producing a much more complete analysis. The same text was input to the pre-editing step with this new list of word parts, and a new set of PTAH runs was made. Input text consisted of 13,410 strings, in 3152 words, on 421 consecutive lines. It may be seen that a smaller volume of text was required to produce about the same number of

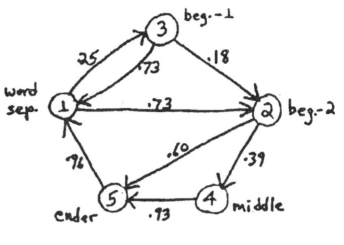

State	1	2		3	4	5
Label	word sep.	begin-ner-2		begin-ner-1	middle	ender
Output Strings	/ (word space)	p 8z 9z bz 4of op 4op es ez ps sq 8	sc of zc z f bs sx ef 8s s 4	4oe zc9 o sc9 4o b oe	cc c ccc c8	c9 89 9 an am aj

UNCLASSIFIED

Fig. 6—State Diagram of Voynich Text Strings: First List (U)

strings as in the first study, due to the more complete decomposition into shorter elements. Also, in contrast to the 225 different elements found in the first word-part analysis, only 81 unique elements were produced, with only 72 having frequencies of 5 or higher.

(U) Figure 7 shows the state diagram, list of states, and some "clusters" of similar elements found by the program at its most restrictive threshold (.005 for this run). The diagram is a bit more complicated, and some of the states have been renumbered, but the five states are basically similar with respect to the associated output strings. There are ten major transitions, compared to eight in the previous study, and two pairs of states are linked by reciprocal transitions. The state diagram in Fig. 7 was deliberately constructed so as to facilitate comparison with Fig. 6; for the most part, there is surprisingly little essential change. The main differences are the following:

a. The strings associated with the states have been slightly altered, in ways that seem to me to improve their consistency and to bring them even closer in line with what I expected, based on my subjective "feel" for recurrent units in the text. More elements that I guessed might be similar are together in the same state, and few if any that seemed well placed in the first word-part results have been lost in the second.

b. There is a new cycle of reciprocating transitions between "beginners-2" and "middles," reflecting the curious linking behavior of the common "c" sequences.

c. There is a new transition from "beginners-1" directly to "enders" and the arrow from "beginners-1" to "beginners-2" has disappeared. This appears to reflect the better separation of common short words from longer words.

d. The "beginners-1" state has a new, relatively low-probability transition to itself, probably occasioned in part by the inclusion of the single symbols "r" and "e" in its output set.

e. In general, far more of the information in the text has been utilized, and the "noise" from the many "leftovers" in the first analysis has been removed (at the possible risk of adding a different source of "noise" in the single symbols).

f. The "clusters" in Fig. 7 are smaller sets of word parts which the program found to be especially similar. They were generated by the program through an analysis of the final output matrix and comparison of the probabilities there. This list of twelve tight clusters is striking in contrast to a list of twenty-eight much more diffuse and multiply-intersecting clusters produced by the first word-part study at the same threshold value (.005). Striking parallelisms between symbols that look alike will be apparent to anyone familiar with the Voynich text (e.g., b, f, and p all followed by s and z; "4of" and "4op"; "of" and "op," etc.).

(U) *Conclusions from the Word-Part Studies.* I find these analyses even more convincing in confirming the highly regular positional structure of elements in Voynich text "words." In addition, these results suggest that the meaningful elements are not words as wholes, or single letters, but larger, variable-length sequences of symbols. Early codes and ciphers in use by the Catholic Church show many instances of such mixed-length elements (single symbols and two- or three-letter units intermixed, some standing for plaintext letters and some for common words and phrases). It is interesting to note

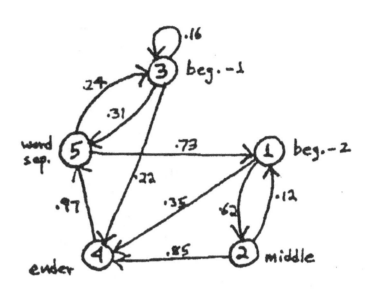

State	5	1		3	2	4
Label	word sep.	begin- ner-2		begin- ner-1	middle	ender
Output Strings	/ (word space)	4of	op	4oe	c	aj
		z	of	2o	cc	89
		4op	f	e	a	an
		es	x	r	ccc	9
		bs	q	o		am
		ez	8	4o		ar
		sx	8s	b		3
		ef	9z	oe		m
		8z	bz	or		ad
		s	sq	o8		
		p	vs	z9		
		oef	4oef			
		9f	ps			
		4	2z			

UNCLASSIFIED

Fig. 7—State Diagram of Voynich Text Strings: Second List (U) that the number of unique word parts found in the second study (81) is very close to that required if Voynich text elements were assumed to stand for plaintext consonant-vowel syllables after the fashion of a syllabary. A 16-consonant list appropriate for Latin (b, c, d, f, g, j, l, m, n, p, q, r, s, t, v, x) in combination with the five vowels (a, e, i, o, u) would provide 80 syllabic symbols. Of course, some convention would be required for the representation of closed syllables and consonant clusters, but this problem is readily solved in many known syllabaries (Japanese phonetic representations for foreign words, for example). It is interesting to speculate that the "ligatured" symbols in the Voynich script might stand for Latin consonant clusters; a similar ligaturing approach to clusters is used in the Devanagari syllabary of India.

(U) We are fortunate in having a PTAH study made by _____ applying PTAH to the symbols of a known syllabary: the "Linear B" syllabary used in Greece and the Aegean Islands around the middle of the second millenium B.C. [7]. This writing system, originally thought by many to embody the records of the Minoan civilization, was deciphered in 1953 by Michael Ventris and John Chadwick to reveal an early form of Greek, similar to that of the Homeric epics. Thus, it provides us with a very interesting parallel to the situation I have hypothesized above: a language involving consonant clusters and closed syllables, written down in a syllabary designed for a language having only open (VC) syllables. Figure 8 shows a state diagram adapted from the phonetic portions of the seven-state PTAH model on page 35 of the reference. (I urge the interested reader to examine this highly readable and informative paper in its entirety.) I have omitted the two states for numeral signs and ideographic signs, leaving a set of five states for word-divider and vowel-consonant syllables which may be compared to our five word-part states for the Voynich text.

(U) The diagram for "Linear B" phonetic signs shows nine transitions, with a clear positional structure very like what we have seen in Figs. 6 and 7. Word-separator is followed by "beginners"; these are followed by "middles-1" or "middles-2"; either of the two "middle" states can lead to the other or to the "ender" state, which in turn leads to word separator. While I will not attempt to make too much of this comparison, and offer it only for its suggestive value, it is still quite striking. When we recall how different the English and Latin five-state models for single letters and the five-state model for code groups appeared, the similarity between Figs. 6, 7 and 8 seems to support a guess that short plaintext word parts may underlie the Voynich script. The distribution of word lengths in the text provides additional support: few words are as long as seven or eight symbols (and these often contain the medial "c" sequences), while many common words are only three, four, or five symbols in length. This picture is quite unlike that in Latin or English written in an alphabet of single letters, where the

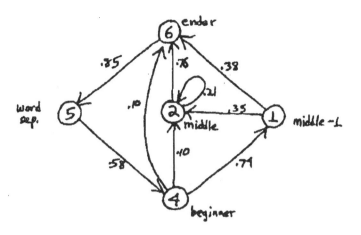

UNCLASSIFIED

Fig. 8—State Diagram of Five-State Model for "Linear B" Syllabary (U)
(adapted from Reference 7, p. 35)

range of word lengths includes many of ten to fifteen characters or more, and there are a great number and variety of seven- and eight-letter words.

4. SOME GENERAL CONCLUSIONS (U)

(U) In closing, I will state some conclusions that I have drawn from these analyses. At the risk of appearing overly positive, and alienating some other students who are convinced that they have found the secret of the Voynich manuscript, I will couch these statements in a relatively unequivocal form.

(U) 4.1 The plain text directly underlying the Voynich text is probably not a natural language represented by an alphabet of single letters like the English alphabet. A PTAH five-state model for single letters of an agglutinative language such as Turkish would provide an additional interesting test.

(U) 4.2 As a corollary, the encryption or concealment system in the Voynich text probably is not any form of simple substitution on an alphabet of single letters like the English alphabet.

(U) 4.3 The Voynich text probably does not represent a natural language, written in an "impressionistic" way (to recall a statement by Dr. Robert Brumbaugh, who claims to have deciphered it as a misspelled, distorted form of Latin), nor can its characteristics be explained by hypothesizing many variant spellings of the same words in an alphabetic writing system (cf. older forms of English). Its structure seems far too ruly and regular to accord with these views. Rather than a distorted or degraded form of English or Latin monographic structure, it seems to exhibit a DIFFERENT structure of its own.

(TSC) 4.4 If the Voynich text conceals a code, it is not very like the example examined above in section 3.2 (a code involving a partially inflected Romance language comparable in some ways to and descended from Latin, and a code in which grammatical endings were represented by code groups: a situation I had considered to be quite close to that called for by Friedman's and others' guesses about artificial languages underlying the Voynich text.)

(U) My intention here is not to attack other students, or to "put down" their opinions; rather, it is to stimulate new research. I have no thought of "clearing the field" for some cherished claim of my own about the Voynich text; I wish to emphasize the fact that I have no single "pet" theory about the manuscript. As others also have said, it is hard to imagine any directly underlying natural language plain text whose characteristics can explain the phenomena adequately. My hope is that this paper, if it has no other impact, will at least provoke some others to approach the puzzle of the Voynich manuscript with some of the modern scientific tools at our disposal, in addition to the intuitive and subjective methods chosen so predominantly by earlier researchers.

5. REFERENCES (U)

[1]

[2]

[3] R. L. Cave and L. P. Neuwirth, "Hidden Markov Models of English," *IDA-CRD Working Paper 239* (January 1969). (U)

[4] M. E. D'Imperio, "An Application of Cluster Analysis to the Question of 'Hands' and 'Languages' in the Voynich Manuscript," *PI Informal No. 3.* (June 1978, S-216,867) and *NSA Technical Journal*, Vol. XXIII, No. 3 (Summer 1978), pp. 59-75. (U)

[5] M. E. D'Imperio, "New Research on the Voynich Manuscript: Proceedings of a Seminar" (Washington, D.C. 30 November 1976). (U)

[6] M. E. D'Imperio, "The Voynich Manuscript: An Elegant Enigma" (National Security Agency/Central Security Service, 1978). (U)

[7] J. Ferguson and H. E. Kulsrud, "Statistical Studies on Linear B," *IDA-CRD Working Paper 441* (January 1975). (U)

[8]

Appendix 1: First List of Voynich Text Strings (U)

word-sep.	cc
line-end	ccc
2o	ef
2oef	ep
2of	es
2z	ez
4o	fs
4o8	fz
4oe	o8
4oef	oe
4of	oef
4op	oep
89	of
8s	oj
8z	op
98	or
9f	ps
9z	pz
ad	rz
ae	sq
aj	sx
am	vs
an	z9
ar	z9f
at	
bs	
bz	

UNCLASSIFIED

Appendix 2: Additions for Second String List (U)

a3	sc	zcp	zf
a6	scf	zcq	zp
au	scp	zcx	zv
92	scq	zcb	zb
29	scx	zcv	sf
9p	scb	zq	sp
9q	scv	sq	sv
9x	zc	zx	sb
9s	zcf	sx	rs

UNCLASSIFIED

An Application of Cluster Analysis and Multidimensional Scaling to the Question of "Hands" and "Languages" in the Voynich Manuscript

BY MARY E. D'IMPERIO

Unclassified

This paper presents the results of an exploratory study of representative portions of the Voynich Manuscript applying cluster analysis and multidimensional scaling to Currier's Hypothesis. Techniques employed are: PEP-1 Guttman-Lingoes Graph Theoretic Algorithm, Ling's (K, R) Clustering Algorithm, HICLUS Agglomerative Method, TAXMAP-2 Clustering Program and the MINISSA Multidimensional Scaling Program.

I am reasonably certain that few readers of this paper will require much of an introduction to the topic of the Voynich Manuscript. Brigadier John Tiltman's informative and enjoyable presentation on 17 November 1975, and the seminar on 30 November 1976 served to familiarize many with this cryptanalytic challenge from the late Middle Ages. There have also been several articles on the subject in *Cryptolog* during the last few years.[*] For any reader who desires an overview of the topic and a summary of some recent research, I recommend the Proceedings of our 1976 seminar [4] a copy of which may be obtained from M. D'Imperio, R53/P13. Two presentations by Captain Prescott H. Currier constituted high points of that occasion: in them, and in the supporting paper printed as Appendix A of the Proceedings, he set forth his theory that there were several different scribes involved in the production of the Voynich Manuscript, and that their individuality was attested not only by characteristic "hands," reliably distinguishable by eye, but also by statistically distinct "languages." If this hypothesis could be confirmed, it would provide students of the Voynich Manuscript with an important new insight into the problem. This paper describes the results of an exploratory study of Currier's theory using cluster analysis and multidimensional scaling.

---

[*]For a description of the MS and reproductions of some of the text and illustrations, see John H. Tiltman, "The Voynich Manuscript—The Most Mysterious Manuscript In the World," *NSATJ*, Vol. XII. No. 3 (1967), 1–45. See also Mary D'Imperio, *The Voynich Manuscript: An Elegant Enigma* (in press).

It has another purpose as well, primarily tutorial, in that I felt a detailed description of an application of these techniques to a relatively clear-cut problem might prove useful to others considering them for use in operational contexts.

CURRIER'S HYPOTHESIS

The Voynich Manuscript is a rather long document, comprising some 210 pages of writing in an unknown script liberally interspersed with colored drawings of a wide range of subjects and exhibiting (at least to us, today) a highly bizarre nature. The manuscript is considered to contain several sections, presumably dealing with different subject matter, as judged by the nature of the drawings. A long initial "herbal" section is profusely illustrated with representations of fanciful plants; an "astrological" section shows zodiacal diagrams and many illustrations featuring stars, suns, moons, and other cosmological elements; a "biological" section is marked by strange associations of naked female figures and objects like pipes, pools, and platforms; other sections are similarly distinguished by their illustrations. Currier's findings concern contrasts he has seen between sets of pages in certain sections of the manuscript, leading him to classify the pages into subgroupings: an approach quite different from that of other students of the manuscript, who almost invariably consider it the monolithic production of one author.

Here are a few highlights drawn from Currier's exposition of his theory at the 1976 conference:

> "The first twenty-five folios in the herbal section are obviously in one hand and one 'language', which I call 'A'. . . . The second twenty-five folios are in two hands, very obviously the work of at least two different men (A and B). In addition to this fact, the text of this second portion of the herbal section (that is, the next twenty-five or thirty folios) is in two 'languages' (A and B), and each 'language' is in its own hand. This means that, there being two authors of the second part of the herbal section, each one wrote in his own 'language' . . . Now with this information available, I went through the rest of the manuscript . . . and in four other places I discovered the same phenomena I associated with 'language' B . . . . The biological section is all in one 'language' (B) and one hand." [4, p. 20 f f.]

While he finds indications of different hands and "languages" in other sections of the manuscript (the pharmaceutical, astrological, and "recipe" sections), these seem much less distinct and clear-cut. It should be noted that in using the word "language" in this context,

Currier does not necessarily mean to imply that he has found different underlying natural languages (e.g., Greek as against Latin, or German as against French). He is referring to patterns of statistical characteristics that seem to be consistently associated with Hand A as opposed to Hand B: certain symbols are more likely to occur together or to appear more frequently in certain positions in the "words" of the Voynich text in folios showing one hand than in folios showing the other. An inspection of his extensive monographic, digraphic, and trigraphic counts and his studies of symbol clusters in various positions of a "word" have convinced him of the presence of at least two clearly distinct bodies of text. In these two corpora the symbols show certain consistently different and characteristic distributions, associated with the visible differences in writing style and formation of symbols marking the hands of two different writers (writer A and writer B). Currier refers to the two bodies of text as "languages" A and B. In summing up his findings, he indicates that he feels quite certain of at least five, and perhaps as many as eight, different hands in the manuscript as a whole, but only two statistical "languages."

This, then, is the exciting hypothesis put forward by Currier. Several of us, after attending his presentation, confirmed his suggestions to our own satisfaction by replicating his original procedure of choosing some pages showing obviously different writing styles in the large herbal section (where the contrasts between scribes A and B are especially striking) and by verifying both the consistent differences in hand and certain clear accompanying differences in symbol patterns. Nevertheless, since so many other approaches to the problem posed by the Voynich Manuscript have been fraught with subjectivity and self-delusion, it seemed important to place Currier's findings on a more objectively demonstrable and secure basis, and to attempt to confirm or disconfirm them by an independent statistical study.

CLUSTER ANALYSIS

In considering statistical tools for investigating Currier's hypothesis, I decided upon that of cluster analysis as an appropriate method. Cluster analysis algorithms are available as computer programs and are widely employed in the social and natural sciences for classifying collections of objects into subsets based on similarities and dissimilarities with respect to a list of scores or observations. The methods can also be used to reveal which of a group of objects is most like another single object in the group. So long as a set of observations has been made, such that every object under study has been scored, rated, or labelled for all the same properties or "variables," the clustering techniques can be applied to reveal subgroups among the objects.

Within each cluster, objects are more like each other than like objects in other clusters. This methodology seemed to me a good choice for revealing the sets of similar pages within the Voynich manuscript that Currier's theory called for, if in fact they were present. For the reader interested in knowing more about it, a number of more or less readable works are available. Cluster analysis has been investigated by R51 for possible applications to Agency problems, and two excellent survey papers by Douglas A. Cope provide a summary of various clustering algorithms [3], and multidimensional scaling and related techniques [2]. A number of good reference works are available in the open literature; two I found particularly useful were Everitt 1974 [5] and Anderberg 1973 [1].

There are numerous ways of carrying out cluster analysis, and the published computer programs embody various combinations of these, considered by their designers to offer some special advantage for certain applications. In general, however, the analysis involves the following stages: 1) deciding upon a group of objects that constitutes a good sample of the groupings or clusters hypothesized by the analyst; 2) deciding upon the observations to be made across all the objects; 3) taking the measurements, scores, rankings, labellings, etc., of each object with respect to each observation; 4) choosing a measure of "distance" (dissimilarity) or, alternatively, a measure of association (similarity) appropriate to the case; 5) computing the distances (or associations) between each object and every other with respect to the observations; and, finally, 6) applying the clustering algorithm to the triangular matrix of distances or associations resulting from step 5. The clustering procedures may be "agglomerative" (beginning with one object and iteratively joining other objects to it to form a cluster, as if crystalizing around a nucleus), or "divisive" (starting with all the objects in one big group and successively splitting them into dissimilar subgroups until no further splits can be made). Within the agglomerative methods, there are further choices among methods of linking new objects to existing clusters: "single linkage" methods focus upon the dissimilarity between nearest neighbors in a cluster, "complete linkage" methods upon the dissimilarity between the farthest neighbors, and "average linkage" methods upon the average dissimilarity among neighbors. As might be imagined, some methods are better at stringing out objects in long, thin chains, while others are better at dealing with globular clumps.

Unavoidably, as in the case with many sophisticated statistical tools, there is a real danger of imposing spurious structure upon the data if the techniques are badly chosen or unintelligently used. A factor analysis or multidimensional correlation method will find "factors" of some sort in any data, however difficult they may be to interpret or put to use. Similarly, a cluster analysis will always find clusters, and it is up to us to pay attention to the indications of significance (the relative compactness of the clusters, the strength of their internal "bonds," and the relative distance between clusters) as shown by the statistical measures which the programs provide as a part of the printout. The interpretation of cluster analysis results is unavoidably circular; we propose a certain structure in the group of objects under study, we perform the computation, and we are happy if we see what we expected, or at least something that makes sense in terms of our original hypothesis, however revised. If the clusters we get bear little or no relation to any groupings we expected to see, and we can make little sense of them in the context of our understanding of the problem, we have some indication that our hypothesis about clusters in the data was not confirmed, but an attempt to reason from such unexpected and apparently meaningless structures backwards to the data may prove unrewarding.

I will not attempt here to go into the details of the cluster analysis algorithms or the various methods of computation; I urge the interested reader to consult the references mentioned above. Instead, I will provide some varied examples of applications in which cluster analysis has proven useful, as a means of communicating the "flavor" of these methods. A frequent use of cluster analysis is in studying the genetic similarities among species of plants or animals, based on some set of chemical or physiological properties. Cluster analysis has been employed in statistical pattern recognition, to discriminate printed letters, geometric shapes, or other visual forms. In archaeology, it has been used to classify groups of artifacts gathered by surface collection over a site; clusters of similar objects concentrated in certain areas within the site were found to indicate different human activities ("women's activities": cooking, spinning, making pots, vs. "mens' activities": weapons manufacture, hunting, herding). A particularly interesting application of cluster analysis to Egyptian Archaeology, published in a recent issue of *Science*, deserves special mention [6]. I will describe it at some length, since it demonstrates so dramatically the usefulness and power of this methodology when intelligently employed.

In 1898, a large cache of Egyptian royal mummies was found in the Valley of the Kings; these mummies, having been plundered and damaged by tomb robbers, had then been gathered together by a later Egyptian ruler, rewrapped, and deposited in two new hiding places. In the process of reburial, the identities of certain mummies were obscured (at least for the modern archaeologist). One in particular, referred to by archaeologists as the "elder lady," or more objectively, as Egyptian Museum Catalog Number 61070, was particularly interesting, since it appeared from certain evidence (e.g., the position of the hands) to be that of a queen. It was suggested that this lady might be Queen Hatshepsut or Queen Tiye (mother of the heretical pharaoh Akhenaton). A set of coordinated studies were undertaken, including data from conventional full-body x-rays, standardized x-rays of the head known as "cephalograms," and scanning electron microprobe comparison of hair samples known to be from Queen Tiye and those from the unidentified mummy. Several different cluster analysis algorithms were applied to sets of scores obtained from cephalogram studies of the unknown lady and ten other mummies of Egyptian queens. The analysis showed clearly that the head measurements of the unknown matched those of Queen Tiye's mother more closely than those of any other queen. This finding was strongly supported by the close match between the hair samples known to belong to Queen Tiye (and obtained from a keepsake in the tomb of another family member) and hair from the unidentified "elder lady".

APPLICATION TO VOYNICH MANUSCRIPT PAGES

Selecting the objects. I was fortunate enough to have at my disposal a large corpus of text from the "herbal" and "biological" sections of the manuscript, transcribed according to the alphabet designed by Currier for computer processing of the Voynich symbols. Currier stated that he had found no page to be broken by a change of hand or "language," so that a set of samples, each taken from the text of a single page, should provide an appropriate test of Currier's theory. I selected forty segments of text, consisting of the first 350 to 400 characters from each of forty different pages. According to Currier's view, the text of these pages should fall into three major classes: herbal pages in "language" A and Hand A, herbal pages in "language" B and Hand B, and biological pages in "language" B and Hand Z. These three classes will be called Herbal A, Herbal B, and Biological B for short in the remainder of this paper. Figure 6 shows a summary of pages from which samples were chosen.

Making the Observations. I decided upon a simple monographic frequency count as a good starting point, since Currier had found a clear difference in the distribution of individual symbols between "languages" A and B. I made forty monographic distributions, one for each of the selected pages, including roughly the first 350 to 400 characters on each sample page (many pages did not contain more than 400 characters, and I wished the samples to be more or less equal in size).

Choosing a Measure of Association. Since my data consisted of frequency counts applied to a set of mutually exclusive, exhaustive events (the symbols of the Voynich script "alphabet") I could avoid the many scaling and normalization problems afflicting investigators employing cluster analysis for sets of observations comprising disparate measurements. My frequency counts constituted a set of discrete, countably infinite or finite variables, on a scale having a zero point and permitting proportional measurement (i.e., if xi and xj are two counts within one distribution, we can say that xj is n times as large as xi). Therefore, I could consider my analysis to involve a "ratio" scale, the strongest of the four possible scales (ratio, interval, ordinal, and nominal) on which observations can be made. This left me free to use a wide variety of cluster analysis programs, employing various association measures. The analysis takes place in the context of a sort of abstract "measurement space" or "metric," within which the objects (manuscript pages represented by frequency distributions) are "located" at various "distances" from each other to form the clusters. Different programs may use any of several possible associa-tion measures, among them the Euclidean distance measure, the "city-block" distance measure (both measures of distance, or dis-similarity), and the correlation coefficient (a measure of similarity).

Computing the Association Matrix and Clusters. Through the cour-tesy of Douglas A. Cope, R51, I was able to obtain runs of four different cluster analysis programs and one program for multidimensional scaling. These programs were as follows: the PEP-1 Guttman-Lingoes Graph Theoretic Clustering algorithm; HICLUS (Hierarchical Clustering), an agglomerative method using single and complete linkage; TAXMAP-2, an average and single-linkage approach to mode-seeking; Ling's (K, R)-clustering Algorithm, a hierarchical K-linkage method; and MINISSA (Minnesota-Israel-Netherlands Intergrated Smallest Space Analysis), the multiple scaling program. These programs have all been adapted for the CDC-6600 computer by Mr. Cope and his colleagues, and are described in his papers [2, 3]. His ingenuity and helpfulness to users in applying the techniques to their problems and interpreting the results have also been a major asset.

I needed only to supply a hypothesis and the set of forty frequency distributions, and the programs then carried out all the computations of associations, finding the clusters, and providing statistical estimates of confidence for the strength of the clusters or the program's representation of the data. In general, each of the cluster analysis programs found a lower triangular matrix of associations (correlation coefficients in PEP-1, HICLUS, and the (K, R) Algorithm, and city-block distance in TAXMAP). Each association in the matrix measured the relation of one Voynich Manuscript page, as represented by its monographic counts, to another single page. Transformations were then applied iteratively to the rows and columns of this matrix so as to emphasize the similarities and differences between pages. In some cases, the programs actually shuffled the rows and columns to bring like objects closer together in a final output matrix display; this was true of the (K,R) algorithm. As each cluster was found, a confidence measure was computed and associated with it in the program output as an aid to interpretation. The MINISSA program employed a somewhat different statistical model of the data; instead of finding clusters of objects in an abstract "space," it mapped the "locations" of the objects within such a space: a "Euclidean metric space," whose two dimensions may be assigned a meaning in relation to the hypothesis held by the investigator.

Interpreting the Results. Many programs provide a helpful graph or plot of the numerical results; in some cases, additional programs can be run on the outputs of a clustering algorithm to rearrange matrix rows and columns or provide graphic displays to aid the researcher. These visual representations are extremely helpful, and I found them almost necessary; unadorned lists of cluster members, ranged in dense rows down the pages of printout, can prove tedious and confusing indeed to the researcher. Since both the clustering and multidimensional scaling techniques are essentially applying a spatial model or "metaphor" to the problem posed by the investigator, a two-dimensional graph or plot is often an appropriate display. Another useful display is a "tree" or "dendrogram" showing the familial relationships among the objects. Each program provides statistical measures, associated with the clusters, the nodes of a dendrogram where each cluster is split off, or with the entire representation of the data. These measures are intended to enable the researcher to assess the confidence he may have in the findings of the program. In the next section, the outputs of the five programs will be described in detail.

RESULTS OF THE ANALYSIS

1. *PEP-1 Graph Theoretic Algorithm.* PEP-1 provides a list of clusters in order as each subset of the objects is partitioned off from the rest. A "family tree" (shown in Fig. 1) can be drawn from this output. At each node of the tree where a cluster or a single object branches off, an "edge connectivity probability" is shown; this is an estimate of the likelihood that the split could have happened by chance. Thus, the lower this estimate of probability (on a scale of 0.0 to 1.0), the more confidence we may have in the contrast of the pages in the cluster

against the rest of the pages outside of it. The upper "stem" of the family tree shows a loose sequence of small clusters and isolated pages, all from the Herbal A pages except for two samples, TL and HD (pages 94 and 76), from Herbal B. The tree then separates into two main branches; the left branch seems to correspond roughly to Currier's "language" B, since it contains most of the B pages and none of the A pages; all the Biological B pages are clustered together at the lower left, along with one Herbal B page (59); another Herbal B page (79) is alone, and there is another cluster of seven Herbal B pages just above. The right branch contains the rest of the Herbal A pages and one oddball Herbal B page (sample TE, page 60). The "probability" statistics seem quite low everywhere except in the right branch, where they suddenly jump up from near zero to .5. Thus, this right branch, while strongly split away from the rest of the tree, seems very weakly subdivided, and should probably be regarded as one very diffuse cluster.

2. *Ling's (K,R) Algorithm.* Figure 2 shows two triangular matrices output by the program. The rows and columns of an original "similarity matrix" containing correlation coefficients have been rearranged to place similar manuscript pages closer together and dissimilar pages farther apart. Symbols made up of overstrikes were printed in the cells of the matrix, so that the higher correlations are darker; thus the clusters showed up as darker triangles along the main diagonal of the big matrix. A matrix was produced for each of several "bond sizes" or values of a threshold K applied to links between objects in clusters. Higher levels of K represent more restriction on clusters, and a requirement for more strongly bonded clusters. Thus, for bond size 1 ($K = 1$), every object in a cluster must be joined to at least one other object in the same cluster by a link of the required closeness, and clusters must have at least two members. For bond sizes 2 and 3, every object must be linked to at least two or three others in the same cluster, and clusters must have at least three, or four, members. While higher bond sizes could have been required, the algorithm produced three matrices, one for each of bond sizes 1, 2, and 3. The first two matrices were essentially alike, and were as shown in the left drawing of Fig. 2. Except for four anomalous Herbal B pages (59, 60, 76, and 94), there appear to be three relatively clear clusters corresponding to the three classes of pages Currier's theory calls for: Biological B, Herbal B, and Herbal A. The matrix for bond size 3 is somewhat different; it seems clearly to show only two major clusters, corresponding to Currier's two "languages," with the exception of the three Herbal B pages (60, 76, 94) and one Biological B page mixed in with Herbal A.

HICLUS Agglomerative Cluster Analysis. The output of HICLUS includes a dendrogram in the form of a display similar to a bar graph. Boundaries between clusters can be seen where low points in the graph-like display leave deep columns of white paper between the relative peaks of the clusters. An accompanying page associates sigmages for cluster tightness to each cluster; the higher the statistic, the tighter the cluster. The vertical dimension of the graph shows descending correlation coefficient values, so that objects associated in a cluster at the top have higher correlations, while the correlations decrease down the page. Figure 4 shows a rough redrawing of this bar graph. We see a rather strong cluster on the far right containing seven Herbal B pages; in fact, they are the same seven as appeared in the 7-page Herbal B cluster on the left branch in the PEP family tree. It has a correlation coefficient level of no less than .959, and a sigmage of 5.3. In the middle is the Biological B cluster, containing all the Biological B pages plus two from Herbal B (59 and 79); its correlation level without page 79 is .960, and its sigmage 7.97; with page 79, the corresponding figures are .947 and 8.47. The left half of the graph tails off into a very loose conglomeration of small clusters comprising all the Herbal A pages with two Herbal B pages (60 and 76). Page 94 is alone as an "outlier" (an object not clustered with any other in the set) on the far right.

TAXMAP-2 Clustering Program. While TAXMAP does not provide a graphic display of its results, Mr. Cope kindly ran its outputs through another program to create a two-dimensional "vector plot" similar in appearance to that produced by the MINISSA program discussed below. It should be noted at the outset that TAXMAP, alone of the programs run on my data, did not employ a correlation coefficient as a measure of association. Instead, a very different kind of measure was used: the "city-block" distance. In effect, this means that much of the information in my frequency count data on a ratio scale was disregarded; instead of comparing the profiles of peaks and valleys along the frequency distributions, a much cruder, less sensitive, and perhaps less appropriate measure of distance was used. This consideration may help to explain the differences in the results of TAXMAP as contrasted with those of all the other programs. The only cluster that shows up at all clearly contains ten Biological B pages. The Herbal A and B pages are scattered among small clusters and isolated individual pages in a manner that tells us relatively little that is useful.

MINISSA Multidimensional Scaling Program. Figure 3 shows a drawing adapted from the "vector plot" produced by the MINISSA program. Whatever feature of the metric space is represented on the horizontal axis, it seems to be related to the differences between

Currier's "languages" A and B. The vertical axis is somewhat more problematical; it could pertain to the "subject" difference between Herbal and Biological, or even to the "hand" difference between Currier's Hands B and Z within "language" B. All the Biological B pages fall within a small, compact region in the lower center, which also contains one anomalous Herbal B page, 59. A compact region above contains the same seven Herbal B pages we have seen grouped in a strong cluster by three of the four clustering algorithms. Page 94 is all alone on the extreme right, and page 76 is alone at some distance above and to the left of center, while pages 60 and 79 are around the edges of the Biological B region. All the Herbal A pages are scattered loosely over the leftmost third of the plot. In general, this program, in spite of its reliance on a somewhat different statistical model, appears to confirm the findings of PEP, the (K,R) Algorithm, and HICLUS.

CONCLUSIONS

Figure 5 shows a rough summary of the groupings of pages found by the five programs. Except for TAXMAP, they all seem to reveal the same picture: A strong Biological B cluster including all the Biological B pages along with one Herbal B page, 59; another cluster containing seven or eight of the Herbal B pages; and a loose association of Herbal A pages mixed with the same few anomalous fugitives from Herbal B. The transcribed data at my disposal do not contain a broad enough sampling from all sections of the manuscript to support a full-scale analysis attempting to study all the "hand," "subject" and "language" contrasts. Nevertheless, the results of this exploratory study clearly seem to be sufficiently encouraging to warrant a more complete analysis when more text has been transcribed.

REFERENCES

[1] M. R. Anderberg, *Cluster Analysis for Applications* (Academic Press, New York, 1973).

[2] D. A. Cope, "A Brief Introduction to Multidimensional Scaling and Smallest Space Analysis" (R51, 1978).

[3] D. A. Cope, "Cluster Analysis: Introduction to Models and Methods," S-215,924, *R51/MATH/25/76*, 16 November 1976; also in *NSATJ*, Vol. XXII, No. 2 (Spring 1977)—REISSUE, pp. 71-97.

[4] M. E. D'Imperio, "New Research on the Voynich Manuscript: Proceedings of a Seminar" (Washington DC, 30 November 1976).

[5] B. S. Everitt, *Cluster Analysis* (Halsted Press, 1974).

[6] J. E. Harris, et al., "Mummy of the 'Elder Lady' in the Tomb of Amenhotep II: Egyptian Museum Catalog Number 61070," *Science*, Vol. 200 (9 June 1978), pp. 1149-1151.

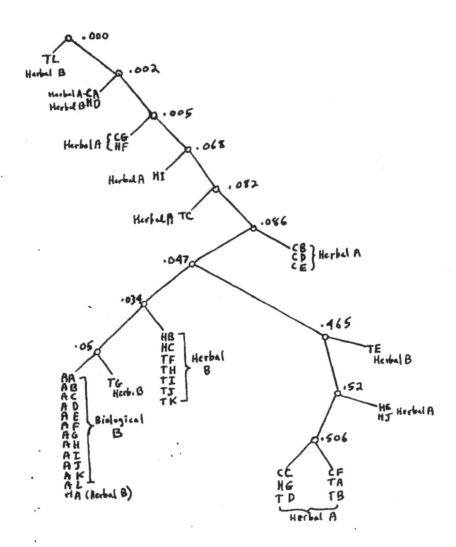

Fig. 1.—PEP-1 "Family Tree" (Single Linkage Clusters)

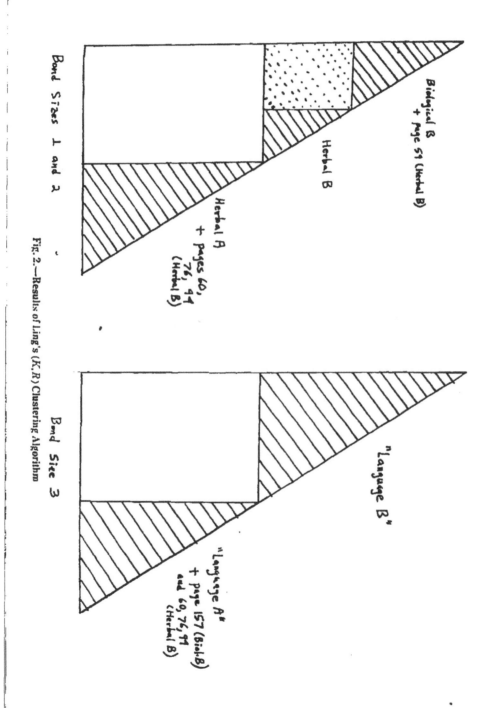

Fig. 2.—Results of Ling's (K, R) Clustering Algorithm

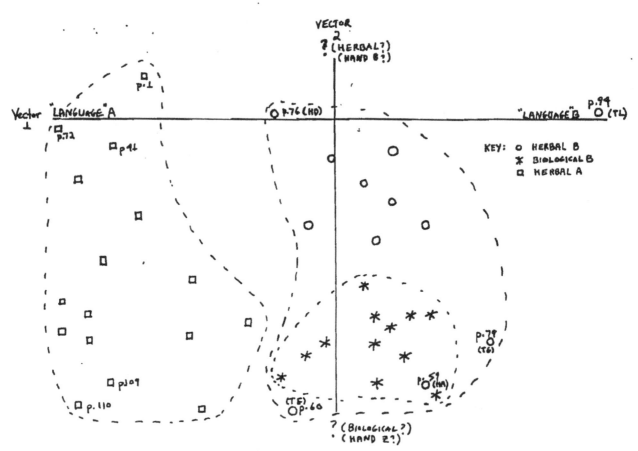

Fig. 3.—Results of MINISSA (Multidimensional Scaling) Program

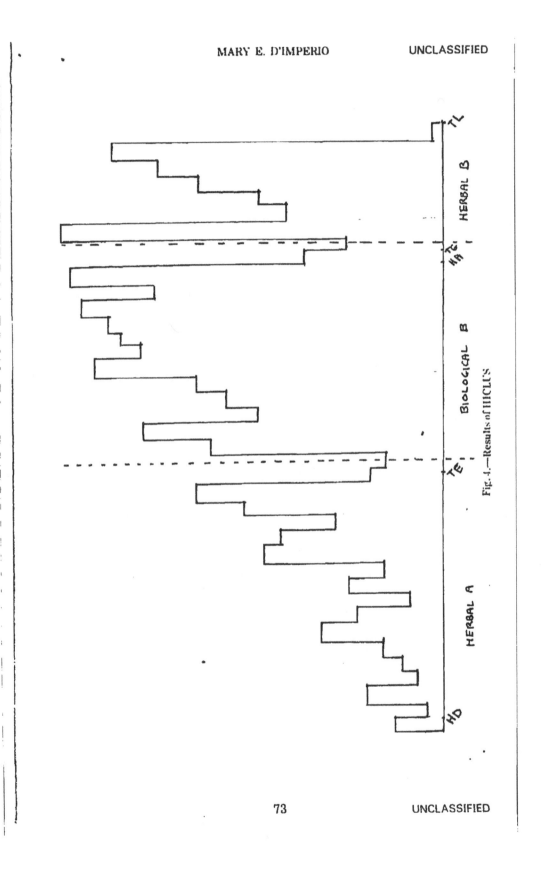

Fig. 4.—Results of HICLUS

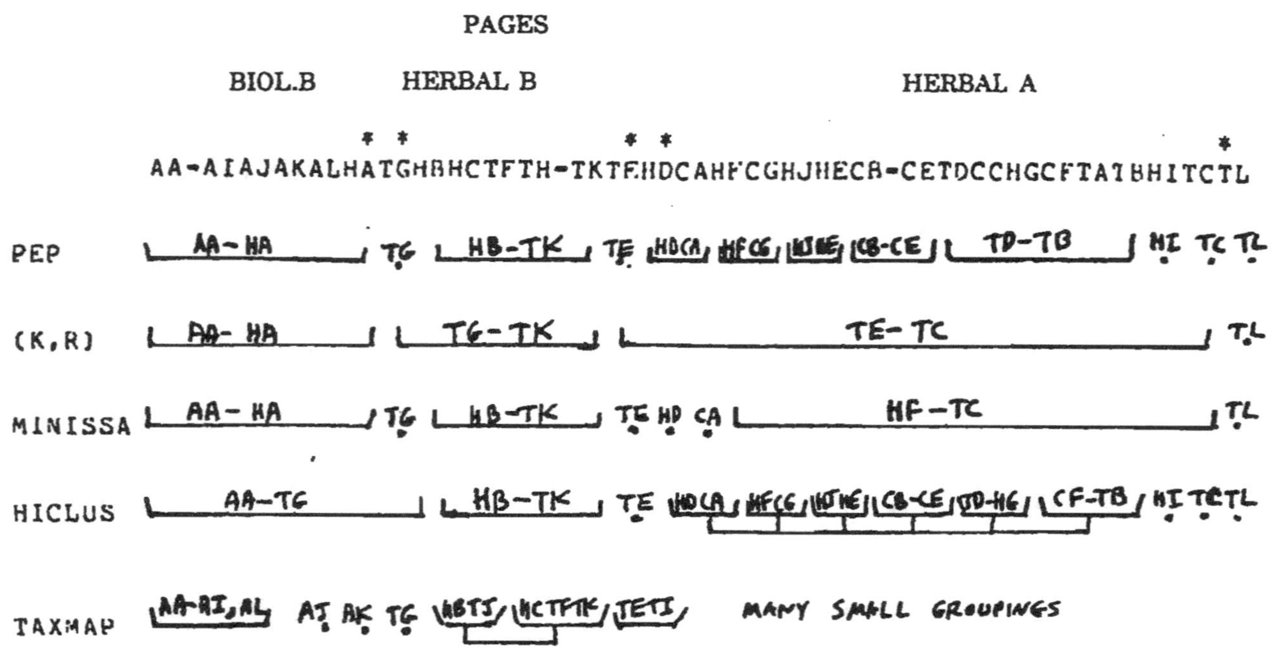

PAGES

BIOL.B   HERBAL B   HERBAL A

* *   * *

AA-AIAJAKALHATGHBHCTFTH-TKTFHDCAHFCGHJHECB-CETDCCHGCFTAIBHITCTL

PEP

(K,R)

MINISSA

HICLUS

TAXMAP   MARY SMALL GROUPINGS

Fig. 5.—Summary of All Program Results

*Indicates Herbal B pages which are sometimes separated from other Herbal B

no.	code	Currier's page no.	"subject"	"hand"	"language"
1	AA	147			
2	AB	156			
3	AC	149			
4	AD	151			
5	AE	148			
6	AF	150	Biological	Z	B
7	AG	152			
8	AH	153			
9	AI	154			
10	AJ	155			
11	AK	157			
12	AL	158			
13	CA	001			
14	CB	005	Herbal	A	A
15	CC	015			
16	CD	032			
17	CE	045			
18	CF	039			
19	CG	041			
20	HA	059			
21	HB	075			
22	HC	065	Herbal	B	B
23	HD	076			
24	HE	068			
25	HF	072			
26	HG	095			
27	HI	110			
28	HJ	081			
29	TA	082	Herbal	A	A
30	TB	057			
31	TC	109			
32	TD	096			
33	TE	060			
34	TF	066			
35	TG	079			
36	TH	083			
37	TI	084	Herbal	B	B
38	TJ	089			
39	TK	090			
40	TL	094			

Fig. 6.—Summary of Samples from Manuscript Pages

75

The Voynich Manuscript Revisited[1]

BY JAMES R. CHILD

Unclassified

In what appears to be an important literary and linguistic discovery, the author begins to remove the veil from "the most mysterious manuscript in the world," the Voynich Manuscript. This brief, tentative, study claims that the Voynich Manuscript does not contain an artificial language nor the enciphered text of an underlying text in an unknown language, but is a text in a hitherto unknown medieval North Germanic dialect.

The Voynich Manuscript, an object of interest off and on since the seventeenth century, contains over 200 pages written in a partially cursive alphabet which has proved indecipherable. Equally enigmatic are the large number of drawings—of plants, few of which are identifiable, and of naked women sitting in tubs or emerging from pipes (one writer has called the latter a "plumber's nightmare").

The history of the manuscript, which has been detailed in other places, needs only passing mention, since it does not throw any light on the content. Dating from about 1500, it was said by Joannes Marci, mathematician and orientalist at the University of Prague, to have belonged at one time to Emperor Rudolf II (1576–1612). Marci writes in 1666 to the Jesuit Athanasius Kircher, in Rome, that he was making a present to the latter of the manuscript, the author of which, he had heard from another source, was the great medieval scholar Roger Bacon. (How Marci came into possession of it, I do not know.)

Marci himself withheld judgment on the attribution, but at least one scholar since his time became intrigued with the notion of Baconian authorship. Professor William Newbold of the University of Pennsylvania was convinced that it was an enciphered text prepared by Bacon and he worked on this assumption from 1919 until his death in 1926. He thought he had deciphered some of it, including an occurrence of "R Baconi" on the last page[2]. His solution has been convincingly refuted by other scholars, who, however, have not offered anything better.

I now rush in where angels fear to tread. Although not a specialist in Old Norse, I am convinced that the manuscript is a text in a

[1] The original version of this paper was received in the *Cryptolog* editorial office 16 February 1976 and was published in the April 1976 issue of that periodical. The present text is a revised version based on further study.

[2] The information in this paragraph and the preceding paragraph was taken from *Horizon*, Vol. V, No. 3 (January 1963).

medieval North Germanic dialect hitherto unknown, at least insofar as the script is concerned. It is not a cipher, and not an artificial language, as has also been suggested. The distribution of vowel and consonant letters, some of which are surely Latin letters, makes a cipher improbable. As for the possibility of its being an artificial language, the linguistic features suggesting a Germanic affiliation render that hypothesis unnecessary.

Most of the manuscript has a depressing number of repeated words and phrases, of little help unless collateral information is available, suggesting that these are prayers, incantations, or formulas of a specific character. This is not the case, unfortunately. I finally chose a mostly unadorned text without too many repeats (Folio 114 recto) to begin with, and a botanical folio (Folio 40 verso) as a follow-up.

I then attempted to find "function" words, that is, connecting words such as conjunctions, personal pronouns, and prepositions, assuming (correctly, as it turned out) that the language would have these. The first item that caught my eye was *o&* , the second letter of which was a mystery. However, I thought the word might be "and" because of its frequent position between longer words which often had the same endings. Remembering *og*, "and," from Danish, I sought out phrases of the type "of mice and men" (Scandinavian literature, like that of Anglo-Saxon, contains many rhyming or alliterative phrases of this type). I was lucky: a phrase in the script form

$$ oo\Upsilon \ldots o\,\ell \ldots $$

occurred. The first is a general Scandinavian word for "from," "out of." This was promising, because not only did the first word appear to be in a known alphabet with the desired meaning, but the second letter of the second word was a tentative recovery ("g"). The same procedure has been of aid in the tentative recovery of proper names, especially those occurring in pairs:

ℋoↄ o& ℋℯℋₑↄᴡ   *Thor og Thruther*
"Thor and [his daughter] Thruther."

Once a few phrases of this kind fall into place, the next logical step is to look for verb forms, and hope that verb affixes and bases of the desired type appear. Again, I was fortunate in finding verbal suffixes and a few high-frequency verbs common in Scandinavian languages: the vowel frequently appears as a suffix on bases which look like high-frequency verbs in North Germanic: *rið-a,* "ride"; *rjoð-a,* "turn red"; *bair-a,* "bear."

The process of trial and error in recovering the letters, which are in some cases digraphs, in the words above was too lengthy for me to detail here, but I am quite sure of their correctness. Further, the suffix -*a* seems to have, according to different syntactic patterns, both third-person plural present-tense and infinitive values, which supports a North Germanic identification. Another suffix, - *oʃ*, seems to be a third-person plural past-tense $\bar{o}$ similar to the -*u* (-*o*) of other Scandinavian languages. If I am correct on this point, the manuscript *ʒ* which I have transliterated as "g," stands for a spirant rather than a stop, and could as well have been rendered "gh" or "h." In this case, the letter could, and I believe did, serve double duty as a consonant and an indicator of vowel length.

From the above it will be clear that this is only a beginning. Spelling "variants" in the manuscript sometimes turn out to be different words and in any case cause difficulties (variant spellings of the same word are common, however, in manuscripts of most Germanic languages, and are not in themselves unexpected). The "letters" themselves are not all recovered, especially those symbols which appear in final position only and which are certainly digraphs in some cases. The inventory of recoveries which are either likely or virtually assured comes to about 15, too few to give a picture of the phonemic structure of most languages. However, several of them must, on etymological grounds, represent two values: *ƌ* for example, stands for both the stop *d* and the spirant *đ*, while *H* may represent the stop *t* and the spirant *th*.

The paucity of identified phonemes need not in itself be a barrier to progress. In Folio 40 verso, a botanical text, judging from the illustrations, I have sufficient values to establish phrase length segments, e.g.,

>   *gotto liđa dagor*, lit.: "having gotten to
>   pass days," i.e., "with the passage of days";
>
>   *tho ir liđa tiđa*. . . "when the time has come. . ."

I have also made tentative recoveries for at least two clauses both of which seem to relate to the flowering of the plant pictured in the folio, but it would be premature to offer a translation.

Obviously a great deal of work lies ahead for myself and others who may wish to pursue the subject. Modern theories of syntax which properly focus on verb-noun relationships in context have made it possible for me to avoid preoccupation with single morphemes. These theories can be of substantial aid to further research.

The single most valuable source for my work has been *An Icelandic-English Dictionary* (Cleasby et al.) which, while out of date in some ways, offers hosts of phrase- and clause-length examples from the literary monuments of Icelandic. Interestingly enough, this is true in spite of the fact that the dialect in question is quite different from Old Icelandic. Naturally, with additional insights from further study,

I will be able to make increasing use not only of other linguistic sources but also of anthropological materials.

BIBLIOGRAPHY

Adolf Noreen, *Altisländische und altnorwegische Grammatik (Laut- und Flexionslehre)* (Max Niemeyer, Halle, 1923).

Richard Cleasby and Gudbrand Vigfusson, *An Icelandic-English Dictionary* (2nd edition with Supplement by Sir William A. Craigie, Oxford, Clarendon Press, 1957).

H. S. Falk and Alf Torp, *Norwegisch-Dänisches etymologisches Wörterbuch* (Carl Winter, Heidelberg, 1960).